The Painter's Craft

A   B   C

D   E   F

BEHAVIOR OF PIGMENTS IN PAINTS

The Painter's Craft

AN INTRODUCTION
TO ARTISTS' MATERIALS

by

RALPH MAYER

Member of the Faculty of Columbia University
and Fellow of the American Institute of Chemists

D. VAN NOSTRAND COMPANY, Inc.

TORONTO   NEW YORK   LONDON

NEW YORK

D. Van Nostrand Company, Inc., 250 Fourth Avenue, New York 3

TORONTO

D. Van Nostrand Company (Canada), Ltd., 228 Bloor Street, Toronto

LONDON

Macmillan & Company, Ltd., St. Martin's Street, London, W.C. 2

PRINTED IN THE UNITED STATES OF AMERICA

PREFACE

This book is designed both as a text for class or workshop instruction and as a guide for the practicing painter who wishes to acquire by independent study a systematic knowledge of the standard data relating to the craft on which his art is based. It presents the basic background knowledge that any artist must have in order to succeed as a competent professional or amateur.

Although planned for the beginner as an introduction to the technical part of artists' work, it should be of much value to the mature painter as an additional source of knowledge, especially when he has not been so fortunate as to have received formal training. The plan and content of the book have been guided by experience gained in a large contact with practicing painters and in courses and lectures given to artists and students.

I have endeavored to confine the present volume to standard materials and procedure, and to avoid those ramifications which lie beyond the compass of a general textbook. After an outline of the important basic principles which underlie the behavior and use of paints, the physical aspects of color are discussed in Chapter 2, solely for their application to the techniques of painting and divorced from any aesthetic involvements. The section on pigments includes only such matter as is essential for a grasp of the subject, yet it omits no important information that the painter should know. The chapters on the various methods or techniques of painting follow the same plan, except that the section on the preparation of gesso panels and also the section on home-made pastels are expanded to somewhat greater detail. One reason for the lengthier treatment of these

vii

topics is that they are typical studio activities and have not, to my own satisfaction, been well described elsewhere. Conversely, the chapter on mural painting has been very much condensed and generalized because, by its very nature, anything less than the most complete volume of detailed information about this subject would not be of much further practical value.

Throughout the book, emphasis has been placed on the basic principles rather than on the "how-I-do-it" method of instruction. Definite recipes and instructions almost always require much alteration to suit individual requirements, variable raw materials, and divergent purposes. The artist who has a sound grasp of fundamentals is in a better position to solve new painting problems more successfully than the one who follows a recipe or set of directions by rote.

The author is indebted to Murray Pease, Harry Carnohan and Bena Frank Mayer for valuable assistance in reading and criticizing his manuscript, to Alvin Taylor and Maurice Bratter for executing the photographs, and to Edward Landon for the preparation of the frontispiece.

RALPH MAYER

Columbia University
September 1948.

CONTENTS

Chapter 1

INTRODUCTION ·

The *craft* of painting is a study apart from the *art* of painting; yet the two are closely interrelated and overlapping. The artist cannot entirely divorce the artistic or aesthetic aspects of his work from his studies of materials and methods by treating the subject on a completely scientific or mechanical basis, nor can he ignore all technical considerations in his efforts to establish a personal technique for the expression of his aims.

However, there are so many different artistic intentions among artists, and so many divergent theories and purposes among groups or schools of thought, that the subject of painting materials and methods must be presented by the teacher to the artist or scholar as a separate technical study, free from aesthetic implications. At the same time, it is understood that few persons will want to study this subject for its own sake; that always behind the effort to become proficient in the media of his craft lies the desire to apply this proficiency to the requirements of the specific form the individual has selected for his art.

Artists and schools of art have strong disagreements and arguments among each other on practically every point concerning the technique of painting, except when it comes to the correct selection and application of painting materials. Here they stand on common ground (or should do so) because the rules of craftsmanship apply equally to the painter who aims at perfection of finish or tight draftsmanship or to the artist who paints in a loose, rough manner; to the one who emulates traditional ideas or to the one whose ideas are in the modern style or of an experimental nature.

The artist must be master of the technical side of his painting for three reasons, all of equal importance:

1. To assure permanent results

If his choice of materials and their application are correct, he will avoid those physical failures and blemishes to which improperly executed paintings are subject with the passage of time. Correct modern procedure is founded on rules and laws, based on scientific and logical principles and substantiated by the experiences of the past.

Permanence in an artist's work means absolute permanence; that is, the work is designed to endure as long as it is humanly possible to insure its survival. It should not be confused with relative permanence, the basis on which our industrial products are designed. Good paints for houses, boats, or signs are expected to wear out and be replaced within a limited period; the difference between a nonpermanent and a permanent industrial paint or varnish is merely that one will fail quickly whereas the other will last for a reasonable number of years before requiring replacement. All the accepted, traditional art techniques in painting are of equal permanence if the pictures are given the care and preservation which works of art are normally intended to receive, except that some are more fragile than others when subjected to more drastic treatment. All of us are familiar with the cracked, blistered or wrinkled condition of some of the old oil paintings or the faded condition of some old water colors. On the other hand, there are many examples of pictures which have remained intact, just as the painter intended them to be seen. We would like our own work to survive indefinitely in good condition, and our only assurance that they will is to follow the established procedures, which are primarily based on knowledge gained from the experience of the past.

2. To secure proper control of manipulations

It is not enough for a paint to be permanent—resisting the ravages of aging and the effects of sunlight, atmospheric conditions, etc.—but, in order to be an acceptable material for artists' use, it must also be capable of being manipulated; that is, it must be under the control of the artist at all times so that the effects which he seeks can be obtained without over-laborious and troublesome procedures. For example, for some styles of painting a paint must be capable of being brushed out thinly and smoothly to a transparent layer which will not sag, drip or run; for others it must be applied in a thicker, more opaque coating. Again, some paints are required to produce crisp, clean brushstrokes; with others a softer, blended effect is required. Also, the color of a paint must be clean, clear, true to its type, and there are several requirements which it must meet in order that the painter may control color effects.

Artists' materials of the highest grade do not necessarily have to be so perfected in these respects that they will respond automatically to any sort of casual or careless attempts to apply them, but they should be sufficiently controllable so that it will not be beyond the ability of the average painter to acquire the skill necessary for successful manipulation after a reasonable amount of experience.

These requirements have not always been in effect. For instance, the very early European easel painters used materials which seem to us awkward and difficult to command. They paid considerable attention to the use of permanent materials, but they overcame difficulties in these matters by developing a very high degree of skill rather than by improving the working qualities of their materials. The later painters either adopted new materials or developed improvements designed to facilitate the executive properties of their paints; by the eighteenth and nineteenth centuries they had even gone so far as to subordinate permanence of results to ease in manipulating paint, or to obtaining special color and textural effects with little or no regard for their lasting qualities.

This led eventually to use of the most impermanent materials and methods; the training and instruction of painters were confined solely to manipulations and aesthetic doctrines, while artists developed their work in ignorance of the most elementary principles regarding permanence. The modern painter has the advantage of improved materials and methods, which have been developed and standardized through the ages and verified by scientific controls, combined with the opportunity to study the basic underlying principles of his craft. This substitute for the earlier apprentice system was either not available or not grasped by many painters of the recent past.

3. To choose appropriate techniques

The choice of a technique which will be most appropriate to the subject at hand, or to the ultimate function of the work, or to the artist's own personal requirements, obviously involves several considerations besides purely technical ones. But the final choice is largely influenced by technical considerations, and the artist who has a broad general knowledge of all painting methods—regardless of which one is his specialty—has a great advantage. He is thereby able to modify and alter his technique to suit his personal requirements by abstracting what he needs from other technical methods of painting; he is also able to vary his technique to suit the different types of painting he may want to do from time to time.

The question of which technique or modification of a technique to use depends on a number of circumstances. A correct decision on this point is quite as important to the artist as his choice of permanent materials, because success or failure in expressing himself depends to a great degree upon it.

Some of our methods of painting are quite flexible as technical processes, with much leeway permitted in the observance of rules and regulations; other methods are more critical and the artist must comply with the letter of the law more strictly.

The intelligent painter will soon learn the common-sense application of materials and methods and with experience will be able to judge for himself. The rules of correct procedure should not be a deterrent to free expression in painting and need not hamper an artist by presenting continual restrictions or bugaboos; rather, they should free him to go ahead and paint with the knowledge that he is doing the right thing. On the other hand, the basic, fundamental rules must not be ignored if permanence and successful manipulations are to be achieved.

The importance of observing all the individual precautions and in following correct procedure in all details may be realized if one considers that frequently a painting is defective or disappointing because of a complication of mistakes. Even in the more flexible procedures, if each one of its elements is a little off, the accumulation of faults will cause a failure, whereas if all the rules have been carefully observed one small error may not matter appreciably.

PAINTS

Painting is the application of color to a surface. This is the simplest general definition that can be made.

Pigments. The colors used in painting are known as pigments. The pigments are dry powders which are manufactured from raw materials (natural and artificial) and which, in order to function properly, must be carefully made to meet very strict requirements. The simplest form of painting, therefore, is to smear dry pigments on a rough surface. This is done in pastel painting; pastels are pigments or mixtures of pigments, molded with water and a little gum into the form of crayons and then dried.

Pigment requirements. The pigments used in the various kinds of paint—oils, water color, etc.—are the same; the difference lies in the vehicle used. This is merely a broad general statement (as will be seen by referring to the remarks about pigments for each technique) since a pigment which is suitable for one kind of paint does not always meet the requirements of another. Some techniques require transparent pigments, some require opaque pigments, and some are limited to the use of pigments with very special properties. All modern methods of painting require a pigment to be a very smooth, finely divided powder, as brilliant and clear in color as its type can be made, free from impurities, and insoluble in its vehicle. It must be absolutely permanent to the effects of sunlight, also of atmospheric and other conditions under which the painting is expected to endure.

Vehicles. Paint, in the ordinary sense of the term, means a fluid material into which a brush may be dipped in order to apply the fluid to a surface and spread it around. Such paints are made by combining dry, powdered pigments with various liquids. When this is done with true pigments of the correct properties, the colors do not dissolve but remain in suspension, completely dispersed in the liquid. After the paint has been applied to a surface and has become dry, the layer of pigment imparts its typical color to the surface; its precise tone, value, or brightness is subject to modifications depending upon the conditions which surround it, these being due mainly to the nature of the liquid used as a vehicle. In practice, virtually no successful paints can be made by a simple mixing of the dry pigments with the vehicle; because for several reasons a paint usually requires thorough grinding by strong friction if it is to behave correctly.

The functions of vehicles. Thus far only one function of the liquid ingredient has been considered—putting the pigment in a fluid form so that it is possible to apply and brush it out. This may be called its *executive* function, but there are three other functions which a vehicle may serve. We could demonstrate the first, or executive, property of a vehicle by using plain water or turpentine as our liquid, which would suffice for this purpose alone, but would result in a spread-out layer of pigment entirely unsatisfactory as a paint. It would be smeary, irregular and dull. When dry it would soon rub off or drop from the surface, since both water and turpentine are completely volatile—that is, they evaporate into the air on drying, and leave no residual substance which has any effect on the pigment.

Binding. If we use a mixture of starch paste and water for our liquid and grind the pigment into it thoroughly, then the paint on becoming dry will hold together, because the pigment particles are pasted or bound into a single mass by the starch after evaporation of the water. This illustrates the *binding* property of a vehicle.

Adhesiveness. However, such a mixture of starch paste and pigment alone does not make a very good paint. The film is very likely to crack and may flake or peel away from the surface because this particular combination of pigment and paste does not have good *adhesive* qualities. If, instead of the starch, we use a glue (made from animal skins), or casein (which is made from the curd of skim milk), or egg-yolk, or gum arabic (a vegetable product obtained from a North African tree), paints can be produced which will have all the three desirable properties: (1) they can be brushed out nicely; (2) the pigment particles will be bound together in a uniform film; and (3) they will adhere well to most surfaces.

Optical. The fourth influence which the medium of a paint has on the pigment is optical in nature; it changes surrounding conditions because, if the pigment is coated or surrounded by the binder (and not by air as it was in the dry state), it will exhibit a different color effect, in conformance with a law of physics. If we make our paint with a well-chosen oil or varnish, the full depth or intensity of the pigment is brought out; the dried layer or coat of such a paint will have color effects different or modified from those produced with a water vehicle even when identical pigments are used. (See B and C, Frontispiece; for further explanation, see page 23.)

Balance of Properties. Not only must paints be mixtures of the best pigments and vehicles, but, in order to meet the requirements of the various techniques, the amounts or proportions of the ingredients must be carefully adjusted; also, the vehicles themselves, which in many instances are mixtures of several components, must be well balanced in order to function properly. Certain techniques are more exacting in this respect than others since the materials required for these must be compounded within very strict limits, whereas the rest allow more latitude both in selection and proportions of the materials used. In the formulation of a paint it is sometimes necessary to sacrifice superlative performance in one direction for the sake of some more important quality. House paint, for example, may often sacrifice permanence and extreme durability because of the deliberate use of materials designed to make the paint act in a certain manner—dry more rapidly, or to brush out easily to a smooth, flawless coat, or to remain indefinitely in a soft, liquid condition on the dealer's shelf. Similarly, it would be quite simple for the maker of artists' paints to produce materials with superlative brushing-out or working qualities, extremely brilliant in color, lower in cost, and exceeding the superficial properties of honest paints—if the restriction of utmost permanence were ignored. Even if a paint has superlative quality in one respect, it is not a successful or desirable material unless it also conforms to all the other required standards. The correct balance of properties for paints will be found listed among the requirements for the materials employed in the various techniques.

Grounds. The nature of the ground or surface upon which the painting is done is of primary importance to the successful performance of all these properties of paints. The role of the ground in relation to the optical behavior of oil paints is noted on page 19, to permanence and adhesion on page 104, and to executive or manipulative control on page 105. The other methods of painting—water color, tempera, pastel, fresco, etc.— also have their very exacting requirements for grounds and supports; no amount of care and attention paid to the paints themselves will give successful results unless the equally important requirements for grounds are also fulfilled.

PAINT QUALITY

We now come to an attribute of paintings which might be said to go beyond the purely technical and to verge on the aesthetic part of painting.

The term *paint quality* describes the intrinsic beauty of a paint coating or the satisfactory material accomplishment of the painter's intentions in paint, as opposed to an inept handling or a paint surface which falls below the accepted standards of good craftsmanship. The term is primarily used in connection with normal oil painting where it implies an acceptably full, substantial paint layer as contrasted with dull or smeary effects; but it may also be used to denote the successful appearance of the paint in other techniques.

Paint quality in a picture is immediately apparent. Some of the elements which contribute toward it are correct choice of materials, reasonably skillful manipulations, and control of color effect. There are no universal laws to which painting must conform in order to get this combination of texture, color and appropriateness because there are so many divergent intentions among painters and because of the different qualities inherent in the various techniques and materials of painting. Painting which is intended to be bold and vigorous demands a different treatment from that in which delicate and subtle effects are wanted. The standards of taste and appropriateness which guide the painter in this respect are not based on arbitrary rules or upon fashion but are universal in their appeal. Ever since the earliest recorded critical estimations of painting as an art form, this attribute of paint quality has been regarded as an essential element of excellence. It is a thing apart from excellence of design or artistry and the most primitive as well as the most refined works may have it or lack it.

Paintings are sometimes greatly appreciated on the basis of supreme accomplishment in a *single* direction—for some aesthetic or emotional element, for qualities of design, form, draftsmanship, color effect, etc., even when they are obviously lacking in other of these attributes, since few important schools of painting have ever insisted on a picture having everything. But few works of art have been held in highest esteem in any period unless the technical possibilities of their *mediums* were exploited to the extent where certain minimum standards of technical excellence were fulfilled, and the attribute called paint quality is always one of these.

Excellence of technique or technical accomplishment also involves a confident, masterly brush stroking and an absence of timidity and "pickiness." All these enter into the creation of paint quality; in fact there is very little in the sum total of our best attempts to establish a good working technique that does not contribute toward that excellence of material which distinguishes successful techniques from those which fall short of their expectations.

Historical Development of Materials

In prehistoric times and from the earliest recorded periods of history, man's use of color—not only for artistic purposes but also for many other functions—has brought about a continual search for pigments and mediums to fulfill the requirements which have been outlined in the foregoing pages. The use of most of the colors and of all the binding materials employed in our traditional techniques is of great antiquity, and scholars have recorded the various developments in materials and methods which have led from early times to our present-day traditions. We have a record of behavior with respect to materials and methods which goes back over two thousand years in written accounts and far beyond that through relics and early examples. These may be studied in the various books on special subjects. (See page 211.) Two of the most complete and well-known treatises that have come down to us are the works of Theophilus Presbyter, a monk who lived in Northern Europe in the eleventh or twelfth centuries, and an Italian painter of the fourteenth century, Cennino Cennini whose book is referred to on page 141. Numerous smaller books and manuscripts of the early days, as well as later works of every period, are available in English translations in art libraries. This study is a valuable adjunct to the painter's understanding of his techniques and bears the same relationship to the techniques of painting as the study of art history does to the practice of art today.

Few painters are interested in following out the exact procedures of the past in order to make exact copies of old masters; a knowledge of the history of materials and methods is useful to the present-day painter primarily because it explains the reasons which underlie the development of our current techniques and because it supplies us with information regarding the permanance and capabilities of our materials.

Development in materials and methods followed the changes and development of art, largely as reflected in the type, nature and purposes of the works of art which were required in various periods; also, it was naturally influenced by climatic conditions and the availability of supplies. Although careful studies have been made both of painting materials from all past ages, and the schools of painting in which they were employed, the average present-day painter still suffers from a lack of fundamental knowledge of his materials, a condition which he inherits from the painters of the eighteenth and nineteenth centuries.

The "secrets of the old masters." As is well known, the early painter received training in craftsmanship in the studio of a recognized master. There, over a period of years, he not only acquired instruction and practice in draftsmanship and painting but he also had duties to perform, arduous tasks and labors in and out of the studio such as were necessary in those days when communications, sources of supplies, ready-made materials and labor-saving devices were rudimentary. He was taught, and gradually entrusted with, the selection of raw materials, the mixing and grinding of paints, the preparation of varnishes, and the making of grounds. He saw these materials consumed, he took part in criticisms, and he thus played an active part in the historical development and improvement of the various techniques. By the time he became qualified to take commissions as a master in his own right, there were few technical secrets hidden from him; and if one studio excelled in any particular technical detail it was not long before its contemporaries could duplicate those results. The handful of masters who are outstanding figures in the history of art were men who combined the common knowledge of their times with extraordinary powers of artistic or creative genius and a high degree of skill.

As conditions changed with the years, a combination of circumstances caused a gradual decline in the basic knowledge of the painter's craft. Gradually earlier studio traditions were abandoned, and by the latter part of the eighteenth century the average artist had changed from a craftsman to a gentleman who had little or no concern with the details of the craft, relying on the shops for materials and, as a rule, confining his entire creative output to whatever single method of painting was in vogue in his particular circles. By the nineteenth century, the lack of permanence and the difficulty of controlling effects had led artists to strive for an improvement in craftsmanship; the most popular of these efforts became a search for the mysterious and elusive "secrets of the old masters." To this day, complicated mixtures of materials and intricate methods of procedure are occasionally invented or unearthed from discarded methods of the past and offered to artists as the means by which the older painters achieved their remarkable results. By employing these systems, the present-day painter is supposed to be able to duplicate such results despite his own lack of skill and training.

Although the level of craftsmanship in painting had reached a very low mark during the nineteenth and early twentieth centuries, it must be remembered that there have always been careful painters who have studied their craft and used rational methods of painting. With our present standardized and improved materials easily available and our present opportunities to study the subject, there is no reason why the conscientious painter of today cannot learn to produce as permanent and controllable results as those of past ages.

Today, a mass of reliable data is available for the guidance of artists who want to improve their techniques or adopt new ones, and the present situation is favorable for experimental work on the development of new techniques. Courses of instruction on practical studio or workshop methods, as well as courses embodying the basic principles of painting technology, are given in various art schools and colleges. Not a very large proportion of those who complete such work—either in educational institutions or independently by themselves—will care to continue all the procedures they have learned, but the knowledge is indispensable.

Few painters, for example, will want to make all their own colors; but, once a painter has learned how they are made, he finds he has elevated himself to a point where he does not hesitate to use his judgment and knowledge in selecting and applying materials to any purpose. There are, of course, certain techniques where it is desirable and profitable to prepare one's own materials; there are some materials which cannot be obtained in any other way; and there are the ever-present emergencies with which artists have to cope. Thus, the ability to make certain supplies or to adapt materials to other purposes can be turned to very practical use.

The Fine Arts Painting Methods

Each kind of painting has its variants or subdivisions, and each is adaptable to a number of purposes. Hundreds of years of experience have shown us that, when preserved under the normal conditions usually afforded to works of art, all are equally permanent, although some are more durable or less fragile than others when exposed to more severe conditions. The principal, accepted methods of painting are listed below:

Oil painting. The typical or customary example is a picture painted in straight oil colors on a stretched linen canvas which has been primed with white oil paint.

Water color. Painting on pure, white, rag paper with prepared transparent water-color paints sold in tubes or pans.

Gouache. Painting on white or tinted paper with the same
materials as water color except that opaque instead of transparent colors are used.

Tempera. Painting on an absorbent gesso ground with
emulsion paints which can be thinned with water. Tempera paints differ from the other water- or aqueous-medium
paints in that they can be manipulated to a greater number of
effects and with more finesse and in that, when dry, they may be
over-painted with other coats of tempera or oil paints without
being disturbed.

Pastel. Painting with pure pigment in the form of crayons
without the use of fluid mediums.

Fresco. Painting on freshly applied, wet, lime-plaster walls
with paint made by grinding the pigments in water. There are
several other less widely used methods of easel and mural painting which will be mentioned in the text.

The accepted techniques of painting have all survived the
test of time because they fulfill certain requirements which fine
arts mediums must possess. In the present period of art there
is far less of the feeling of the recent past that oil painting is
the noblest or most serious form of easel painting and that
water color and the other recognized methods are minor techniques, but each one of these kinds of painting is appreciated
for what it is, a particular method which the artist has chosen
to express his intentions, using the plastic or technical means
most appropriate to his purposes.

SUMMARY

To summarize the basic principles covered in this chapter,
the following points can be emphasized.

1. A paint is made by grinding a dry, insoluble pigment into
a liquid vehicle.

2. A paint vehicle has four equally important functions; the

first concerns the liquid paint, and the other three, the dry paint film.

Executive. The vehicle keeps the paint fluid, so that it can be applied and manipulated as required.

Binding. It holds the pigment particles together in a continuous layer, so that the layer will be strong and durable enough to withstand the service required of it.

Adhesive. It secures the pigment layer permanently to the surface to which it is applied.

Optical. When dry, the substance of the vehicle surrounds the particles of the pigment and thereby alters its color effect, changing it from its original state in which the particles were surrounded by air.

3. A basic rule is that any paint must have balanced properties—that is, it must comply with all of the requirements of its type. Even if it is superlative in one single property, it is not a good or useful material unless it is also satisfactory as to its other requirements. The rule also applies to each component of a painting—a pigment, an oil, or a water medium or the ground on which it is painted.

4. Paints must be composed of time-tested, accepted, thoroughly known ingredients, in order to comply with the painter's three main requirements: permanence, successful manipulation, and appropriateness of materials and method according to the work in hand.

Chapter 2

COLOR

The painter uses color as a direct means to realize his creative expression. In order to control color effects, he must understand certain fundamental technical points regarding the physical behavior of his materials. Color has been studied from many viewpoints; countless books have been written, and many divergent theories and systems have been evolved, covering its various aspects—aesthetic, psychological, purely scientific, etc. In connection with the materials and methods of painting, however, the only aspects of color with which we are concerned are the few fundamental rules of physics and optics which govern its behavior when used as an instrument or tool of painting. Systems of color classification, arrangement, color harmony, etc., are studies apart from the present one.

Although we use color in accordance with the principles of art—or personal interpretations of them—rather than with those of science, there are basic physical facts that we cannot ignore; some familiarity with them, or at least with the consequences or results of the behavior of materials, will aid us in controlling our color effects. The tools and materials we use are physical things; so, for that matter, are our finished canvases and as such they are subject to physical and chemical laws just like any other objects.

Definition. Color is not a standard property of a substance. It is not one of its definite, unalterable attributes such as weight, hardness, or crystalline structure, but is an effect produced by a substance under certain circumstances on the vision of the beholder.

16

A scientific definition of the term color would be that it refers to all sensations aroused in the mind of a normal observer by the response of the retina of the eye and its attached mechanisms to the radiant energy of certain wave lengths and intensities.*

In order to see color, it is not necessary to look at landscapes or people or still-life objects; a blow on the eye or pressure on the eyeball will make you see colors; also, you can see or perceive colors with your eyes shut. Such effects are called stimulus colors.

Pigments and light. When daylight passes through a prism, it is separated or broken up into a number of colored rays, creating the familiar spectrum of rainbow hues. This simple and well-known phenomenon is used to demonstrate the theory that white light is made up of a mixture of these component rays, each one having a definite wave length which can be measured by laboratory methods.

Because of its physical, chemical, or crystalline properties, every substance has the property of selectively absorbing some of these wave lengths from the white light; like a radio set it tunes in on these waves and that is why their hues are different. Ultramarine blue, for example, absorbs all except the blue portion of the spectrum, a percentage of which it reflects back, thus producing the sensation we perceive as blue. Cerulean blue absorbs less of the spectrum; it reflects back together with blue portions, some of the waves which give the green sensation; hence we perceive it as a more greenish blue pigment. Colored bodies do not all reflect the same percentage or amount of light, each one varying in this respect; some are much less reflective than others.

Subtractive and additive color. The mixing of colored paints or pigments comes under the description of *subtractive* mixture, so called because the more hues in the mixture, the more color is subtracted or absorbed from the white light. Each pig-

---

* The word is also used in several other senses; for example, paints, especially artists' paints, are called colors.

ment in the mixture absorbs or subtracts from the white light its characteristic quota, so that only the hues reflected in common by all the component pigments are transmitted to the eye.

The *additive* method of color mixing is a term applied to the mixture of colored beams of light, as if each separate color of the spectrum were focused on the same spot. In the subtractive method a paint mixture of the three primary colors, red, yellow, and blue will produce black. In the additive method the three primaries are beams of scarlet, blue-violet, and green light, which if focused or projected on the same spot will produce white light by being added to each other. It has been said that some small element of this principle enters into the effect produced by the impressionists and especially the pointillists and also in the loose scrambling of paints instead of mixing them intimately. However, the pigments used in such techniques are the same as those in the usual kind of painting, and the blending of tones in the eye of the observer functions on much the same basis as the ordinary mixture of pigments. The subtractive principle of color mixing is the only one that has much practical interest to the painter.

Value. Black pigments absorb virtually all the visible components of light and reflect back little: white pigments absorb scarcely any and reflect almost all. Mixtures of the two, or grays, will perform according to their proportion, and the degrees of reflection are known to the scientist as *brightness* and to the painter as *value*.

Intensity and saturation. The chromatic colors react to light in the same way as do the achromatic colors (black, white and intermediate grays); a pale or light color is one which reflects much white light from its surface, along with the colored rays, while a deep-toned or *intense* color reflects less. *Saturation* is a term which refers to the degree of vividness of hue of a color.

Other technical color terms are defined under pigments on page 31 because their descriptions and their usage are more pertinent to the pigments themselves than to color discussed from a theoretical standpoint.

The Behavior of Light Waves

When beams of white light impinge on the surface of a painting, three things happen to them:

1. Some of the waves are absorbed.

2. Some are reflected, as by a mirror.

3. In the case of transparent or translucent substances, some are transmitted.

Fig. A.

4. In the case of a transparent or translucent layer of paint over an opaque or reflective ground, the diagram looks like number 3 on top of number 2.

Generally all three things happen: some of the light gets reflected by the surface; some is absorbed by the paint; some gets transmitted through the paint where it strikes the ground, the ground absorbs some of it, and the rest is reflected back through the paint film.

One of the most useful and practical applications of these principles is the lesson they teach on the importance of using a brilliant white ground for the majority of painting methods. A white gesso ground, a white oil canvas, or a piece of water-color paper, placed in the sunlight or on a well-illumined wall, will reflect the light brilliantly. If, by some magic, you could retain such a secondary source of light and carry it into a dark room, it would illuminate the room like a lantern. This inner luminosity is what the transparency or glaze painter depends on for his color effects, and it also has a pronounced effect on opaque or body-color painting. Whether the painter utilizes thin areas of paint where it would be obvious, or relatively thick, opaque layers which appear to hide the ground, the effect of a brilliant, white, reflective ground usually has its influence on the final result and is a very desirable and necessary foundation for most kinds of paintings.

Although some of the great masters of the past employed dark grounds at various times and for special purposes, our experience through the ages has taught us that the present rule of using white grounds will usually serve our purposes best and will produce the most satisfactory results.

Gloss. There is also another sort of reflection called *specular* which has to do with gloss and mat surfaces. A highly specular or mirror-like surface will bring out the final degree of intensity or saturation of which a surface is capable. The reflection from a mirror or mirror-like surface is a different sort of thing from the diffuse reflection of light by a less glossy surface, which owes its reflective power to its brightness or whiteness.

Mat or diffuse reflection. Completely lusterless surfaces are called mat or flat finishes. Those with a faint, smooth sheen are called semi-mat or eggshell. A surface which is fairly glossy, but does not have the full, shiny gloss of a brightly varnished or polished area, is called semi-gloss.

A mat finish exists because its surface, instead of being perfectly smooth, is broken up into a texture of microscopic roughness. If you look at a piece of water-color paper under a microscope or a magnifying glass (Figure 1) you will see that instead of a smooth, unbroken surface, it is a mass of interlaced fibers of rough texture. Under the same enlargement, a piece of shiny paper, which has a smooth coating laid over the fibers, will reveal only the minor irregularities of the coating (Figure 2). A coat of water-color or gouache paint has no gloss because its surface is misroscopically rough or granular, made up of myri-

FIG. 1. Water-color paper. (Photomicrograph.)

FIG. 2. Coated paper. The stripe is a silver-point line. (Photomicrograph.)

ads of little grains of pigment and paper fibers. A sheet of glass which has been ground and made translucent instead of transparent has no gloss because its surface is a mass of tiny pits and scratches.

When the light strikes one of these surfaces it does not reflect back directly, as it would from a mirror or from a highly polished smooth surface, but is first reflected back and forth among the myriad tiny facets of the irregular or coarse particles; therefore, the total light which is reflected back from the surface comes from all angles, resulting in a diffuse reflection of light and producing the mat effect.

A water color, gouache, or pastel is mat or lusterless because of the roughness caused by the tiny particles of pigment lying on its surface. A normal oil painting—and especially a varnished painting—is glossy because there is surplus vehicle surrounding or overlaying the pigment particles, encasing them in a film or flowing out to a smooth surface.

If an oil painting or some of its areas dry without gloss, as frequently happens,* it is because the same roughness of surface exists. A number of causes can produce this effect: an over-absorbent ground will drain out the surplus vehicle, as will overdilution with turpentine or overpigmentation in the manufacture of the paint. It can also be produced by the use of a dull coating (see page 106). Because it is obviously impossible to have the thickness or oil content of a paint mathematically uniform throughout the picture, there is frequently a difference in gloss in different spots because the thinner portions or the strokes containing less oil will retain less gloss over an absorbent ground.

Color variation. Color, not being a standard property of a substance, is subject to much variation depending upon the environment or conditions surrounding the material under observation. Several external conditions may alter the color effects of a pigment; for example, the quality and degree of intensity of the light under which it is viewed have a decided effect on the way colored substances look. Painters are familiar, also, with the strong effect on color that is caused by the juxtaposition of other colors—how a color can be altered by changing the colors of the areas which border on it.

The principal cause for variation in the color effect of a pigment, however, is the influence of the medium which surrounds it. If you will turn back to the diagram on page 19, which illustrates the transmission of light waves through a transparent solid, you will note that the beam takes a shortcut as it travels through the substance and emerges at a different angle from that at which it impinged upon the surface. Each substance will impede light to a different extent and this property may be measured.

Refractive index is a term which denotes the numerical degree of this power. When two substances of varying refractive

* This condition is known by the term *sinking in.*

indexes meet, the greater the difference between their refractive indexes, the greater will be the amount of white light reflected at the points where they meet, and the brighter or whiter will be the result. The closer their refractive indexes are, the less will be the reflection of light and the greater the absorption of light at these points; the substance will therefore appear to be deeper or more intense in color. For example, an ultramarine blue, with a refractive index of say 1.50 in the dry state, has its particles surrounded by air (which has an index of 1.00), and looks like illustration A in the frontispiece. The same pigment ground in linseed oil (refractive index 1.48) is a deep-toned, intense color like illustration C, which is not an ordinary color print but an actual film of ultramarine blue in an oily vehicle. The refractive indexes in this case are closer to each other; less light is reflected, and more is absorbed. Illustration B shows what the same pigment looks like when ground in a gouache vehicle—a color effect intermediate between the other two.

In the wet stage a gouache paint looks almost as deep as wet oil paint. On page 95 the change in color effect of a dry pigment being mixed with oil can be noticed, and on page 174 the same sort of change occurs when a pigment is mixed with a water binder. But because the bulk of the gouache liquid (water) evaporates on drying, whereas nearly all the oil vehicle is still present in the dried paint, the appearance of the dried paints is quite different. In the dried oil paint, the pigment is completely surrounded and locked in a film of dried linseed oil. In the water paint, there is no such large surplus of medium present, and there is no corresponding encasement of the pigment in its medium; there is rather just sufficient binder present to bind the pigment particles and hold them permanently to the ground. Consequently the pigment is practically exposed to the air, instead of being surrounded by a relatively thick coating of dried oil. The materials used as binders in water paints are powerful glues or adhesives as compared with linseed oil; hence a very much reduced amount of such binder can be used in water paints.

A familiar example of the effect of diffuse reflection is snow, which appears white because the light is diffusely reflected from the myriads of planes and facets of its particles, whereas its substance (water or ice) when viewed in the mass, is clear and transparent.

Variations in gloss and opacity. As noted in the preceding paragraphs, the same presence or absence of surplus medium, which makes for color variation also accounts for the mat or lusterless finish of water paintings as compared with the gloss or luster of oil paintings. The actual surface of normal oil paint is smooth (even where coarse brush strokes build up the paint to a seemingly rough texture) because it is a natural property of fluid oils and resins to flow out and dry to a smooth shiny surface; whereas all the water paints when dry have such a small percentage of solid binder present that the pigment particles lie virtually exposed on the surface, thus causing the microscopic roughness, which results in a diffuse reflection of light from its surface.

Just as color and gloss are affected, the transparency and opacity of a paint pigment can vary greatly depending on its surrounding medium. Alumina hydrate, which is described under *Inert Pigments,* is an opaque white material in the dry powder state, but if it is mixed with oil, it becomes transparent because the refractive indexes of the oil and the pigment are close.

When surrounded by paint vehicles, pigments of low refractive index are more transparent than those of higher refractive index. As a general rule—to which there are several exceptions in the cases of certain individual pigments—there is also a direct relationship between the weight or specific gravity of a pigment and its opacity. For the most part, the lightweight, fluffy pigments are transparent while the heavy solid ones are opaque.

Variation in intensity. After noting the fact that the color of a pigment in an oil painting is deeper and more intense than that of the same pigment in a painting made with one of the water or aqueous paints, and also the fact that the depth and intensity of a painting is considerably increased by having a high gloss on its surface, it can be seen that full intensity of color effect in an oil or a varnished one may be the result of two conditions: (1) encasement of the particles in a medium of high refractive index; (2) addition of a higher degree of gloss to the surface.

Because our palette is made up of such a heterogeneous collection of substances having a wide range of chemical and physical properties, it would not be natural to expect any one medium to have the same effect on each color. And so we find that there is quite a range of degree in which the various pigments are affected by being surrounded with a paint vehicle; the color effects of some are altered enormously, whereas others are very slightly changed. This point is brought out very clearly in considering the action of fixatives on pastel pictures (page 171); and, as we shall see, it has a definite bearing on the appropriate selection of materials and techniques to achieve desired results.

Conclusions. Thus, besides influencing the color effects of the various pigments, the surrounding medium or vehicle of a paint also determines its other visual properties. The binding vehicles of oil paints, water colors, tempera and gouache paints each combine with pigments to produce paints that have their own individual characteristics; the same pigment which gives opaque effects in one technique may be semi-opaque or transparent in a different paint. The opacity of our most dense pigments can be reduced under certain conditions.

The painter, once he has grasped these principles need not struggle continuously to apply them. By becoming familiar with the individual properties of his various paints and pigments and their behavior under differing circumstances he is free to use them without anxiety or puzzlement, and with the assurance that he can exploit the possibilities of his technique to its fullest extent.

Again the appropriateness of techniques. At this point it is most important to state that the examples used here to demonstrate the principles of gloss and mat effects, as well as the differences of color properties inherent in oil and aqueous paints, are not intended to convey or imply any superiority of one method over the other. Water-color painting can have a beautiful intensity of color within its own range; and all the other techniques have desirable qualities of color, texture and workability each of which is appreciated according to its fitness or to the manner in which it may be adapted to the artist's aims.

Chapter 3

PIGMENTS

Historical. The history of pigments is well documented; studies have been made of all the descriptions from old manuscripts and books dating back to the earliest recorded times. Actual analyses of pigments from relics of prehistoric civilizations and from all later periods have been systematically carried out. The student of the history of painting materials will find that throughout the history of European painting on down to the present day there has been a steady improvement in the quality, variety, and availability of pigments. Our present permanent pigments are superior to those of the past in all respects and are continually being improved. The current existence of fugitive and inferior pigments, which painters must avoid, is a circumstance no different from that of former times; these have existed in all ages and places, and careful painters have always had to know which ones were safe to use.

PROPERTIES AND REQUIREMENTS

The dry powdered pigments, from which artists' paints are made, must conform to several requirements in order to be acceptable for use in painting.

Color properties. Some pigments are characterized by brilliance and depth of tone, others are normally duller or paler, but each should be as clean, clear and bright in color as its type permits. The transparency and the opacity of pigments must also conform to the highest standards of their types.

Pigment properties. This term refers to the significant physical and chemical properties of a pigment other than its color qualities. Paint pigments must be completely insoluble in their vehicles. They must be smooth, uniformly fine powders capable of remaining in suspension in the vehicles with which they are compounded, so that their color, degree of opacity, and general optical effects can be smoothly and evenly applied to the surfaces of paintings.

Permanence. An acceptable pigment must neither fade nor darken on continued exposure to sunlight; it must not be chemically altered or harmed by the action of vehicles or of other pigments with which it comes in contact under the circumstances to which works of art are normally subjected.

The fading (or darkening) of the color of a pigment on exposure to sunlight is a definite chemical reaction, set in motion by the wave lengths to which the pigment is exposed. It is also dependent upon the intensity and the duration of such exposure, and in many cases it will not take place unless other chemical agents are present (for example, water or a moist environment).

All the pigments listed in this book as approved for use in the various techniques of permanent painting are inert to such actions. Only when the paints contain inferior pigments will the colors fade or darken. Some of the permanent artists' pigments can be made to undergo chemical changes (and consequently be altered in color effect) by use of drastic methods, but inasmuch as these paints will resist fading or other chemical changes indefinitely *under the conditions to which works of art are normally exposed,* they are accepted as permanent, light-proof colors. For example, alizarin red is an acceptably permanent artist's pigment showing no color change on normal exposure over long periods of time when used in easel paintings. However, if the same pigment be exposed to a powerful carbon arc machine for some days, a definite change can be induced; also, long and continued exposure to the direct rays of the sun, as on a roof, may have the same effect.

Likewise, other chemical treatments can alter certain pigments. Oil paints made with cadmium yellow mixed with flake white will not darken on exposure to light; but, if cadmium yellow and flake white are taken into the laboratory and boiled together with water in a test tube, the mixture will turn quite dark. For this reason some chemists have stated that these two pigments should not be used together. Paintings, however, are seldom boiled, and so there have been no examples of an oil painting having darkened because of this mixture. Cadmium yellow has been on the artist's palette for more than a century, and flake white for more than twenty centuries. Flake white is on the approved list for oil painting only.

Because all the failures of nonpermanent colors are caused by chemical reactions, it follows that the pigments of the highest degree of permanence are those which have the most stable and inert chemical properties.

Purity. The highest grade pigments are those which have been carefully made, washed free from all removable impurities, and are uncontaminated by foreign substances. The commonest impurities met with in inferior pigments are: inert materials or cheapeners with which the more expensive pigments may be adulterated; native impurities which occur, together with the original earths or stones from which some pigments are made; noncoloring ingredients added, not primarily as adulterants but to improve pigments for uses other than as artists' materials (good colors for ceramic processes, printing inks, house paints, etc., often contain modifying ingredients which make them unsuitable as materials for permament painting).

On the other hand, a pigment is not necessarily a single chemically pure compound, and the name or chemical formula of a pigment does not always mean that the principal substance of which it is composed is its sole ingredient. Frequently, small amounts of modifying ingredients are necessary to develop the full perfection of a color; these are permanent in themselves, are recognized components of the pigment as known under its specific name, and are not considered as impurities.

There are a few exceptions to the rule that all pigments must be concentrated, full-strength examples of their types. Prussian blue, phthalocyanine blue, phthalocyanine green, Indian red and some of the alizarin or madder reds are occasionally improved by the addition of various amounts of inert pigment. The cadmium-barium colors and titanium-barium white, which contain relatively large amounts of barium sulphate, are perfectly acceptable pigments, although the same types are also obtainable and may be used in their concentrated, full-strength forms. The inert ingredients, in these instances, are produced or formed during manufacture, as an integral part of the pigment rather than as a substance added to or mixed with the finished color. Some pigments give dull or inferior results when used full strength in gouache paints and are brightened and improved in paint quality when the correct amount of inert pigment is mixed with them.

Emphasis is always placed on the purity, brilliance, and strength of the color characteristics of a pigment. This does not mean that one must paint all his pictures in an intense, clean, brilliant key, but such qualities are necessary because it is not possible to use color in painting to its fullest complete range and in complete manipulative control unless one has full command of all potential color values and qualities. The pigments provide a tool or means of expressing the all-important element of color in painting, and as such must be of the best available grade, just as brushes, carving tools, etc., must be. The artist who paints in a free, spontaneous or loose manner demands the same high quality brushes as the one who does more precise, meticulous work, and the sculptor who carves rough and direct forms requires the same keen implements as the one who produces smooth, polished work. Likewise, when a painter works in a dull or low color key, he needs the same clean colors as when he paints a brighter picture; in the blending and mixing of hues and tones to produce somber results, purity and clarity of color characteristics play as important a role as they do when bright color effects are desired.

TECHNICAL TERMS

There are a number of technical terms employed in discussing the color qualities of pigments and paints; the following brief paragraphs will define them sufficiently to explain the meanings in which they are used in this book.

Mass or top-tone. The surface or opaque body-color effect of a substance, for example, the mass-tone of burnt sienna, is shown in D of the frontispiece.

Undertone. The color characteristics of a pigment when it has been diluted with much white or when it is spread out to a thin, transparent layer. Undertones of burnt sienna are shown in E and F of the frontispiece; in the case of this particular pigment they are markedly different from the top-tone.

Hue. Hue refers to the generic color identification of a substance; for example, one speaks of a thing as being red, or green, or bluish-gray in hue.

Tint. Tint refers to the modification of a color by the addition of other colors: for example, tinted paper is white paper which has been colored by the addition of a little pigment or paint; the tinting strength of a pigment is its degree of power to color white paint when mixed with it.

Shade is descriptive of a degree of variation in color—for example, a lighter or darker shade of pink, a more reddish shade of purple, etc. In any system of color gradation, a step in the scale may be called a shade.

Tinge refers to a staining or permeating by a color; it usually implies a faint, weak or partial coloration.

Cast is descriptive of a slight complexity or subtlety of color. It may also mean a tendency toward another color, not sufficient to classify it as being a definite shade; for example, two yellows may be of the same shade, yet one may have a slightly reddish cast.

Broken color. The pure hue of a pigment when used in a painting sometimes seems to the painter to be "raw" or garish. He will then tone it down by mixing in other colors, thus modifying it to suit his aims and usually making it more subtle or bringing it into harmony with the general key of the painting. This is called a broken color, in comparison with a pure or bright one. Since the days of the impressionists, another meaning has been attached to this term; mixed color effect produced by the juxtaposition of small strokes of separate colors over an area, instead of by painting in a solid area of well-mixed paint, has also been referred to as broken color.

CP. This designation which in chemical technology means chemically pure, when applied to pigments, refers to full strength, undiluted materials.

Let-down or *reduced* pigments are those which contain inert fillers or extenders.

Nomenclature of Pigments. The artists' material trade has emerged so recently from more than two thousand years of utter confusion in the naming of pigments that many confusing names are still in circulation. The pigment names used in this book are in accordance with standard, accepted artists' nomenclature as adopted by authorities and technical organizations in this and other countries. For complete pigment lists which also include obsolete, discredited, or confusing names and synonyms, the reader is referred to the complete manuals and to old books on the subject.*

Classification of pigments. It is not sufficient for the artist to learn merely the general outline rules about pigments or to be familiar with them only as classified into groups. Because of the wide variation in their individual behaviors and properties, each one must be noted by itself, and its relative position in the general classification must be learned. The most satisfactory way to classify a pigment is according to its source, because most of the significant properties which any pigment groups may have in common can be attributed to their composition.

All paint pigments are manufactured products; regardless of

* An all-inclusive list with an explanatory preface will be found on pages 28–65 of the author's *The Artist's Handbook of Materials and Techniques.*

whether they are obtained from natural or artificial sources, they will never be satisfactory unless they have been carefully prepared by expert methods.

The distinction between "natural" and "artificial" pigments is that the artificial are made by chemical reactions and processes from raw materials which are not in themselves pigments; the natural are refined from native ores or earths by physical and chemical treatments which convert these crude coloring matters into improved pigments with the desirable color and pigment properties.

1. *Native earths.* Highly colored clays, soils and rocks occur all over the world; however, the best types occur in limited districts where superior brightness or clarity of tone or freedom from impurities makes them outstanding, or where there are well established facilities for mining, pulverizing and purifying them economically. The *approved* pigments made from natural earth sources are of absolute permanence for all paint uses.

2. *Calcined native earths.* Upon calcining (roasting in a furnace), the earth colors tend to become warmer or more reddish and in some instances more transparent. The calcined or burnt earth colors have the same high degree of permanence as the raw earths.

3. *Artificial mineral colors.* This term includes a multitude of inorganic chemical pigments both good and bad; no general statement can be made to cover their properties, and the characteristics of each must be learned separately. Some are made by the simple mixture of two solutions of salts which will combine to make an insoluble, colored precipitate; others entail complex processes in several stages; all must be made under expert control. Some of our most permanent colors are among the artificial inorganic pigments, while others are not sufficiently permanent for artists' use. As a general rule, those whose processes include a high-temperature furnace treatment are the most permanent of all.

4. *Organic pigments.* (The chemical term *organic* refers to compounds which contain carbon as one ingredient.) These are almost always of a complex nature. A large number of brilliant pigments are made synthetically from aniline which is a coal-tar product; they are widely used for industrial purposes and range in permanence from very fugitive colors to some of fairly good stability, but none are entirely satisfactory for artists' painting. According to general consensus of opinion, none of them has been proved sufficiently reliable, by actual experience over a period of years, to be employed in works of art. A few of the modern aniline colors, greatly improved in lightproof qualities over those of the recent past, have sometimes been made into artists' materials and recommended prematurely; however, it is wiser to adhere to the generally accepted list, at least until more conclusive evidence has been established in their favor. The only two synthetic pigments of organic composition which have been given universal approval for all easel painting use are the alizarin and the phthalocyanine pigments, neither of which is an aniline derivative. The older organic pigments, refined from natural plant or animal coloring matters, are no longer widely used; they are, as a general rule, inferior in all respects to the aniline colors which have replaced them in industrial use.

One of the most serious defects which disqualifies most of the organic colors for use by artists is their property of *bleeding,* or becoming soluble in the oil paints which surround them. If a scarlet lake, for example, were used in an underpainting and white were painted over it, the scarlet would "strike through" the white, staining it. The same thing would occur if the white were painted next to it, and it occurs when painting over an old underpainting as well as over recently dried paint; the color actually permeates and travels through contiguous paint.

5. *Lakes and toners.* The lake colors are made by fixing or precipitating a water-soluble dyestuff upon an inert pigment (see page 56); the process is similar to dyeing cloth. Few lakes

are permanent enough for artists' use. A toner is a concentrated form of lake, made with little or no inert pigment.

THE PERMANENT PALETTE

In the following list, the *hue designations* in the left-hand column comprise a complete palette such as the average painter customarily uses. The right-hand column lists all the completely approved pigments used in oil painting. Painters in water color, gouache, tempera, pastel and fresco have a somewhat smaller choice of pigments available in some of these categories because some of the pigments which are entirely acceptable for use in oil paints have properties or shortcomings which make them undesirable to use in the other methods of painting. References to such exceptions will be found in the chapters which deal with these techniques.

White............... Flake white
                     Cremnitz white
                     Zinc white
                     Titanium dioxide
                     Titanium-barium white

Black............... Ivory black
                     Lamp black
                     Carbon black
                     Mars black

Dull red............. Indian red
                      English red
                      Mars red
                      Burnt sienna (also listed as a brown)

Bright red........... Cadmium or cadmium-barium light,
                      medium and deep (maroon)

Transparent red....... Alizarin reds

Blue................. Ultramarine blues
                      Cobalt blue

Greenish blue......... Phthalocyanine blue
                   Pale greenish blues:
                      Cerulean blue
                      Manganese blue

Dull yellow.......... Mars yellows
                   Yellow ochres
                   Transparent ochres
                   Raw sienna

Pale bright yellow..... Cadmium or cadmium-barium yellow, pale
                      Strontium yellow

Deep bright yellow.....Cadmium or cadmium-barium yellow
                      medium, deep and orange
                      Naples yellow
                      Transparent bright yellow:
                      Cobalt yellow

Green................*Bright greens:*
                      Viridian
                      Phthalocyanine green
                   Dull greens:
                      Chromium oxide
                      Cobalt green
                      Green earth
                      Ultramarine green

Brown...............Burnt umber
                      Raw umber
                      Burnt sienna (also listed as a red)
                      Transparent brown:
                      Burnt green earth

Violet...............Mars violet
                      Cobalt violet
                      Manganese violet
                      Ultramarine red

A painter seldom uses more than one pigment from each category in the same picture, but when he needs them he has a sufficient variety and choice to fulfill all his color requirements among the permanent pigments. His choice and the number of colors he uses depend on his personal preferences and on the requirements of the particular work at hand. A working palette which contains less than a dozen colors can be considered a simplified palette, whereas one in which more colors are used would be a full or elaborate palette.

Restricted palettes. Successful painting can be done with a palette limited to a very few colors and on some occasions a simplified palette can be employed to considerable advantage, for there can be several valid reasons for using a small number of colors. However, in the majority of cases it is most advantageous technically to have a full range of pigments available. Single pigments are invariably purer, more brilliant or vivid than mixtures of pigments made to imitate them. Uniformity of effects and an economy of effort are a few of the other advantages of using colors whose hues are close to those wanted in the final effect.

Painters receive training with simplified palettes as a matter of discipline; sometimes the exigencies of circumstances compel the use of a small assortment of colors, and often a painter will deliberately adopt a limited palette because he finds it best serves certain aesthetic reasons, aims or principles. But even in this case it is not wise for the mature painter to exclude too rigidly from his palette pigments which he does not habitually use, but which on occasion can be introduced into a painting with good results.

The pigments which comprise our modern approved list are the survivors of a process of elimination which has been going on for a long time—actually, for thousands of years. They remain in popular use not only because they fulfill the necessary chemical and physical requirements but also because a long development has established their status as good and useful tools of coloring and because each has individual characteristics sufficient to warrant it perpetuation. Neither artist nor colorman wishes to include or perpetuate an excessively large number of unessential items, and therefore it can be assumed that the colors on the approved list are all valuable.

DESCRIPTIONS OF ARTISTS' PIGMENTS

White pigments

White lead. Flake white and Cremnitz white are the two names under which white lead is sold to artists. They are both basic carbonate of lead, but are made by different processes and have somewhat different crystalline or physical properties. The choice between them is a matter of personal preference, the difference between them being small. White lead, one of the first artificially manufactured inorganic pigments, has been used since the earliest recorded days, and until comparatively recent times was the sole white pigment used in oil painting. It is a dense, heavy, opaque pigment and, when mixed with black or with the chromatic pigments to make pale tints, imparts a more generally pleasing tone than do other whites. When used in oil paint, it has perhaps the finest mechanical or physical properties of all the pigments. It absorbs less oil, it brushes out better, it dries rapidly, and it produces paint layers of superior permanence and durability. Its two defects are: its poisonous nature and a tendency of its surface to turn brown when exposed to sulphur-bearing fumes. Lead poisoning can be avoided by observing the simple precautions of cleansing the hands and fingernails thoroughly after its use, and by not breathing the dust from the dry powder. It is poisonous only when swallowed or inhaled—its danger has been somewhat overrated in the recent past. The same precautions should be observed with all paints, as there are other pigments which are undoubtedly harmful when taken internally. Examples of well-painted oil paintings darkening because the white lead was affected by sulphur are extremely rare; works of art are seldom exposed to such conditions. Although flake and Cremnitz whites are valuable oil colors, they are never used in pastel, water color, fresco or any other purely water medium, because in these techniques the two disadvantages mentioned are more serious considerations. They are, however, sometimes used in tempera painting when the picture is overpainted, glazed or varnished, but not in straight tempera which is unprotected by an oil or varnish coating. White lead will brush out poorly in water mediums as compared with the other whites. The commercial white lead in oil, sold in paint stores, is not suitable for easel painting but may be used in grounds.

Zinc white. Pure zinc oxide made by the so-called French process has been in use for more than a hundred years and has replaced white lead for many purposes. Under the name of Chinese white, it serves as the principal white pigment used in water color and gouache. It is a snow-white pigment, and when tinted with black or other dark colors it yields cold tones as compared with the comparatively warmer, generally more pleasing tones obtained with white lead. When ground in oil, it loses a great deal of its hiding power, and the artist's zinc white oil color is generaly rated as semi-opaque. Sometimes this property is advantageous, but it is usually to be considered a disadvantage as compared with white lead. In physical properties zinc white in oil is distinctly inferior to white lead. It brushes out with difficulty, it dries very slowly, and its film tends to become brittle. However, it is free from white lead's two defects. It is not poisonous, and if exposed to the action of sulphur fumes no darkening takes place because the products of any such reactions would in themselves be white.

Titanium whites. Pure titanium dioxide and titanium-barium pigment have been sold as artists' materials since about 1920. Both kinds have approximately the same physical properties and are equally acceptable as chemically permanent pigments, but the pure oxide is more opaque and has greater tinctorial power than the titanium-barium pigment—so much so that its great tinting strength in relation to its bulk is likely to cause it to be awkward to handle. The titanium pigments are dense and heavy and have great hiding power. They are absolutely permanent and chemically inert. They do not react with oil; for that reason they do not form such intimately mixed pastes with oils, and so are less likely than lead or zinc whites to mask any after-yellowing or darkening of the film. When used alone, titanium does not produce the most permanent or durable of oil films; in industrial paints it is usual to mix 40 per cent to 60 per cent of zinc oxide with titanium, thereby producing a film which has more durability than either one alone. Titanium pigments give their best results in water mediums. Their greater inertness to oil may cause fluid paints to settle out in the containers more rapidly than when white lead or zinc is used.

Mixed white. A mixture of zinc and titanium whites, ground in oil and combining the desirable characteristics of both pigments, is preferred by some painters, mainly on account of its special brushing or executive properties. Because some white paints sold under this name may contain undesirable additions, a brand which conforms to the Commercial Standard (see page 207) should be selected. The pigment components of such paint will be stated on the label.

BRUSHING QUALITIES OF WHITE OIL PAINTS

Choice of white oil paints depends largely on their brushing or manipulating qualities. The upper portions of the four samples illustrated were applied with a full bristle brush to show average heavy brush marks, the curved strokes at the right show the effect of full impasto or loaded strokes, and the lower portions were more thinly applied and were smoothed somewhat by repeated stroking with the brush.

Figure 3. Flake white ground in oil.

Figure 4. Flake white in oil made more fluid with an addition of glazing medium (page 112.) Brush marks have a tendency to flow and become less sharp.

Figure 5. Flake white ground in sun-thickened linseed oil. Stroked to show some of the rugged textures it can produce; effects reminiscent of Rembrandt's paints can be created.

Figure 6. Zinc white in oil. Less facile than flake white and less conducive to paint quality. Effect of brush stroking is harsher; repeated stroking with the brush tends to give crumbly, plowed-up rather than smooth effects.

Red pigments

Red iron oxides. The unstandardized and rather confusing nomenclature of the red iron oxide pigments makes it desirable to consider them all under one heading. There are two distinct types: (1) the bluish variety usually known as *Indian red* which produces rose pinks when mixed with white; (2) the scarlet type known as *English red* or *light red* which produces salmon pinks when mixed with white. These pure iron oxides, artificially made in furnaces, are absolutely permanent for all techniques. They are dense, opaque, and have good tinting strength and pigment properties. Many special shades of pure iron oxides from bright reds to deep crimson and maroon tones are also made under the name of *Mars reds.*

The pure red oxides have their counterparts in a large number of native red earths produced in various parts of the world. These contain varying amounts of inert material, and for artist's use they are now almost entirely replaced by the modern pure oxides.

Vermilion (mercuric sulphide). Vermilion is a dense, opaque bright red, the heaviest pigment in use. In Greek and Roman times a native ore called "cinnabar" was used, but later, when processes for chemically manufactured vermilion became available, the duller, inferior native product was discarded. Vermilion is usually considered one of the oldest chemically produced pigments on the artist's palette.

For centuries vermilion has been accepted as a permanent pigment for easel paintings, but in recent years some doubt has been expressed as to its permanence to light under all conditions because of an inexplicable tendency in some instances to turn dark or revert to the black form of mercuric sulphide. Although these occurrences are not frequent, they have hap-

FIG. 3.

FIG. 4.

FIG. 5.

FIG. 6.

pened often enough so that some very careful painters have replaced vermilion with the completely reliable cadmium reds.

Cadmium reds. The cadmium reds have been available for paint use only since 1919 but their pigment properties are well known; they are identical with those of the century-old cadmium yellows, and the cadmium reds are universally accepted as being completely reliable for all easel painting purposes. The light shade is a perfect replacement for vermilion; the medium, dark and maroon shades are also valuable but, as a general rule, painters make less frequent use of them. Two types of cadmium reds are on the market, the CP or pure cadmium sulpho-selenides and the cadmium-barium reds. The latter grade is considerably less expensive, although it is the equal of the CP grade in permanence and in all other properties except tinting strength, in which respect it is considerably weaker. The cadmium reds are brilliant in the dry state and are densely opaque.

Alizarin reds. These are bright, transparent lakes made in a limited range of tones, all with a characteristic crimson mass tone and a bluish undertone which yield clear rose pinks. Although not absolutely permanent under drastic test conditions, this red is sufficiently stable to be accepted as a permanent pigment for easel paintings under the normal preservation of works of art, and its performance in this respect serves as a sort of minimum standard to which other pigments must conform to be accepted in artists' palettes. It is superior to the old rose madder lakes which have lasted for centuries when not exposed to extremely destructive conditions. Alizarin is made synthetically from anthracene, a coal-tar derivative, and replaces the older madder lakes which were made from a root, the active coloring matter of which contains alizarin. Modern improved alizarin may be freely combined with any of the other pigments on the approved lists without harmful effect. By mixture with other pigments or dilution with glazing mediums, it can be made to match any desired color effect which could be produced by the older, less satisfactory red lakes of vegetal or animal origin.

Inferior and obsolete red pigments. Harrison red, lithol red, scarlet lake, geranium lake, para red, and American vermilion are names for aniline lakes which fade on exposure to light and which are likely to bleed in oil.

Cochineal, carmine, lac, and crimson lakes are products of insect origin. All are fugitive; they have long been discarded, and alizarin replaces them.

Venetian red, originally a native earth but now a deliberate mixture of iron oxide with various percentages of calcium sulphate (a substance harmful to the durability of oil paints), is replaced by Indian, English and Mars reds.

Dragon's blood, logwood, and Brazil wood are antiquated lakes of vegetal origin, replaced by alizarin.

Bole or Armenian bole is a red earth of the clay type, now used only to make grounds such as are used for water-gilding on panels, picture frames, etc.

Blue pigments

Ultramarine blue. This is now the principal blue pigment used in all paints; it is of absolute permanence in all techniques except fresco. Before 1828 the rare and costly native ultramarine, which is refined with great difficulty from lapis lazuli, a semi-precious stone, was in use. Ultramarine is a furnace product made in a number of grades and in a variety of tones, but the usual kinds sold as artists' material are more or less uniformly characteristic. The special types of ultramarine which have distinctly different tones are always designated by different names such as "Imitation Cobalt Blue," "Ultramarine Violet," etc. Ultramarine blue is illustrated in the frontispiece.

Cobalt blue. True cobalt blue (Thenard's blue), a furnace product, is absolutely permanent for all uses. Its hue is of the same general type as ultramarine, but in paints, its top-tone is considerably lighter and brighter while its undertone is greenish compared with the violet or reddish undertone of ultramarine blue.

A dried layer of true cobalt blue ground in oil has one color peculiarity which it displays only in unvarnished oil paintings after they have been exposed or aged. The color becomes whitened, losing its depth of tone, as though it had faded. Upon varnishing such a whitened cobalt blue, the color is immediately brought out again in all its original tones. None of the other permanent pigments has this action to such a degree—it is a sort of exaggerated "sinking in."

Cerulean blue. A furnace product which is absolutely permanent for all uses. Unlike the other permanent blues, cerulean blue has a solid or earthy quality. Other blues owe their hiding power to their deep, dark hues, rather than to their solidity. Cerulean blue has a distinctive deep azure or sky blue top-tone and is quite greenish in undertone. It is expensive, and therefore a cheap paint which is labeled "cerulean blue" is likely to be either an imitation or an adulterated product.

Manganese blue. Although long known and appreciated as a reliable permanent pigment, economic or practical considerations have confined this color until recently to the status of a laboratory rarity. Its mass-tone is similar to cerulean blue but considerably cleaner and brighter; its undertone is very greenish.

Phthalocyanine blue. The most recent of the permanent pigments (1935), this intense and powerful blue differs greatly from the other blues; its color is similar to that of Prussian blue. It has been entirely approved for use in all easel painting methods; many artists find it a good substitute for Prussian blue in mixtures. Because of its coppery bronze sheen and poor pigment properties, also because of its unusually high tinting strength, a grade reduced to about 25 per cent with inert pigment is preferable for most uses to the CP grade. The pigment is a complex organic compound (copper phthalocyanate), a product of modern synthetic chemistry.

Inferior and obsolete blue pigments

Smalt. Replaced by cobalt blue.

Egyptian blue. Permanent, but not available. Replaced by cobalt blue, cerulean, and various mixtures of permanent pigments.

Bice. Copper carbonate, replaced by cerulean and cobalt blues.

Azurite. Replaced by cerulean and cobalt blue. Was formerly a water-color pigment made by pulverizing the native stone.

Indigo. As an artists' pigment, an obsolete and unreliable vegetal color, now made synthetically. It can be matched by a mixture of ultramarine and phthalocyanine blues.

Prussian blue. Long included in artists' lists as a "borderline pigment," which meant not entirely or reliably permanent but reasonably so, and was considered indispensable because of its distinctive color effect. Now replaced by phthalocyanine blue.

Yellow pigments

Ochre. An earth of the clay type which contains varying proportions of hydrated iron oxide. Ochres occur all over the world, but the best are mined and refined in France. Ochre is permanent for all uses, and it is one of the oldest traditional artists' pigments, used in all techniques. When strongly heated in a furnace, yellow ochre turns red, but the burnt ochres and light reds thus produced are no longer used to any great extent, having been replaced by the more intense red oxides. The usual ochre is very opaque.

Transparent gold ochre is refined from a rather rare species of ochre. It is permanent, and suitable for all painting uses.

Raw sienna is a purified and refined native earth similar to ochre but semi-transparent and of a deeper and more subtle tone. It contains small amounts of manganese in addition to the iron. It takes its name from Siena in Italy where the early supplies were obtained. It is produced in various parts of the world, but the best grades still come from Italy.

Mars yellow. This pigment is a permanent artificial iron hydroxide which bears the same relation to the ochres and raw siennas as the pure Indian, English and Mars reds do to the native red earths. Brighter, clearer, and several times stronger in tinctorial power than ochre or sienna, it is preferred by many painters for these reasons, while others prefer the more subtle tones of the traditional earth colors.

Mars yellow, yellow ochre, raw sienna, all have distinctive color characteristics which make one preferable to another for certain uses, but an artist will seldom require more than one yellow of this type in the same palette.

Cadmium yellows are produced in a wide assortment of shades from a pale primrose to a deep orange. They are permanent for all artists' techniques except fresco and are dense, opaque, smooth pigments. The modern grade, labeled "cadmium-barium" yellow or orange, is just as permanent and satisfactory but is definitely less powerful in tinting strength than the more expensive CP or pure cadmium sulphide yellow.

Further remarks descriptive of cadmium yellows will be found on page 44 under *cadmium reds,* with which they are identical insofar as pigment properties and permanence are concerned.

Naples yellow is lead antimoniate, a permanent, opaque pigment used only for artists' oil painting and having the same attributes and defects as white lead. By itself, and in mixtures, it gives pleasing tones which cannot easily be duplicated by substitution. Like white lead, it has fine brushing qualities, produces paint films of superior durability, and is well liked by painters. It should not be used in water color, gouache, pastel, or fresco, or in straight tempera; however, Naples yellow is used in tempera if protected by oil glazes or varnish. The same restrictions that govern the use of white lead (page 38) also limit the use of Naples yellow.

Its hue is a subtle yellow of medium shade and brightness;

sometimes variations either toward the pinkish or greenish are available, but usually its color is uniformly characteristic. Naples yellow sometimes has the peculiar property of turning to a muddy green when rubbed with an ordinary steel palette knife. When a stainless steel or a new polished blade is used, however, this does not occur.

Strontium yellow is a pigment of clear, very pale, rather greenish shade, permanent in all techniques except fresco. It is sometimes useful to produce the palest lemon or primrose hues, as well as light greens of a different quality from those which can be made with other yellows. It has a fair degree of opacity, but in comparison with the cadmiums it must be rated as semi-opaque.

Cobalt yellow (aureolin) is permanent for all techniques except fresco and is one of the most expensive pigments in regular use. Although it has some small degree of hiding power and opacity, it is definitely a transparent pigment as far as practical use is concerned. Its top-tone or body-color when applied in a thick or impasto manner is a muddy tan and it is of little value when so used; but, when applied in thin glazes or as a tinting color, it is a very useful, transparent, bright yellow. It is the only completely approved transparent yellow in modern use and replaces such obsolete and fugitive pigments as Indian yellow, yellow lake, gamboge, etc.

Inferior and obsolete yellow pigments

Chrome yellows and oranges. Heavy, opaque pigments made in a great variety of shades and produced in large quantities for industrial use. The chrome yellows are not lightproof, turning dark or greenish on exposure. They are replaced perfectly by the cadmiums. Chrome yellows contain lead; they must not be used in pastel, water colors, or children's paints.

Indian yellow, gamboge, yellow lakes, Dutch pink, stil-de-grain and other obsolete transparent yellows of inferior permanence are replaced by cobalt yellow.

Zinc yellow and barium yellow are "twins" of strontium yellow as far as color is concerned. Although of a fair degree of permanence, zinc yellow has been excluded from most modern lists of artists' pigments both because it is slightly water soluble and because it is likely to turn greenish on exposure. Barium yellow is an acceptable pigment, as permanent as strontium yellow but so pale in tone that strontium yellow is universally preferred. It can be matched perfectly by adding white to strontium yellow.

Modern transparent yellow lakes sold under such names as Hansa yellow, Monolite yellow, Sunfast yellow, etc., have been recommended by some manufacturers but have not been completely accepted by impartial authorities, either because they may bleed in oil or may react with other pigments. By reason of their recent development, practical or definite proofs of their reliability have not been possible.

Green pigments

Viridian. Introduced in the middle of the nineteenth century, this pigment has become the chief green on the artist's palette. It is a furnace product (chromium tetrahydroxide) and absolutely permanent for all artists' techniques. It has a clear, transparent emerald hue, but heavy impasto layers in full-strength are likely to appear blackish and dull when dry.

Its principal uses are for clear, transparent oil glazes and water-color washes, and for producing all sorts of greens and blues through mixing with other transparent or opaque pigments in all techniques. It serves well as the sole green on a limited or restricted palette. In oil painting it is safer not to use it full strength in undercoats, because such layers are not particularly strong and contain a large percentage of surplus oil. It is a bright green in oil only when mixed with paler pigments or applied thinly over them.

Green earth. A clean, clear pale green pigment, it is permanent for all paint purposes, but so transparent, and so low in hiding and tinctorial power when ground in oil, that its usefulness is confined to glazes and transparent painting of a rather olive hue. In opaque water mediums such as gouache, its body-color or top-tone is a pale hue of the celadon or willow green type. It was used traditionally in Italian fresco and tempera for underpainting flesh tones; in aqueous mediums its color effect has always been a favorite with artists.

Chromium oxide green. A rather dull, cool willow green and a high-temperature furnace product, it is absolutely permanent for all pigment purposes. It is a heavy, dense pigment with fair opacity but rather low tinting strength. Although it is somewhat limited in usefulness and range of effects, chromium oxide is well liked by artists.

Cobalt green. This pigment is a furnace product, absolutely permanent for all techniques. It is somewhat brighter, clearer and more bluish than chromium oxide green, but similar in general properties. Not widely available.

Phthalocyanine green. See phthalocyanine blue. The green is a chlorinated variant of the blue and its pigment properties are identical. Its hue is similar to that of viridian but considerably more intense. Its tinting strength in the pure state is enormous, and therefore it is customary (and permissible) to use a grade that has been reduced to about 25 per cent.

Ultramarine green. A permanent green variant of ultramarine, which has the same properties as ultramarine blue, it is extremely weak in color and tinting strength, resembling green earth in this respect and consequently has very limited uses.

Inferior and obsolete green pigments

Emerald green. A brilliant, bright, rather light green which cannot easily be duplicated by mixtures of other pigments. Permanent only when used in oil by itself, and when well varnished. Likely to turn black when mixed with most other pigments except titanium or zinc whites. A highly poisonous material, it is sold as an insecticide under the name of Paris green. Must not be used in pastel, in water paints, or in children's paints. Seldom used by modern painters. It has occasionally been confused with *vert emeraude,* a French name for viridian.

Verdigris, malachite, green bice are obsolete copper pigments of doubtful permanence easily matched by mixtures of other colors.

Chrome green. An intimate mixture of Prussian blue and chrome yellow. Large amounts are used in industry and many different shades are produced, but the pigment is not permanent for artists' use. Chrome yellows are perfectly replaced by cadmium yellows, and when various shades of the cadmiums are mixed with phthalocyanine blue or green, permanent colors can be obtained to match the hue of any variety of chrome green.

Brown pigments

Umber. The best quality umbers are mined in Cyprus and are known as "Turkey" umber. They are permanent, opaque enough for most purposes, and at the same time sufficiently transparent when spread out in thin layers to serve in all techniques of painting. Burnt umber is more reddish in mass-tone than raw umber, which—in direct comparison with it—seems greenish.

In oil painting, both raw and burnt umber act as powerful driers and yield tough, flexible films. They absorb large amounts of oil and therefore, in conformance with the recommendations and precautions against the cracking of oil paints (page 99), should not be used full strength or approximately full strength in underpaintings; whites or other pigments of lower oil content may crack if laid over them. The umbers are not entirely satisfactory in those mixtures where the very deepest or darkest colors are attempted, because of their tendency to impart chalky or whitish effects to such mixtures.

Burnt sienna is one of the most useful and versatile pigments on the artists' list, as an opaque pigment for its top- or mass-tone, as a tinting color, or as a glaze color for transparent effects. Its color effect is clearer and less chalky than that of most other earths and it serves well in dark or deep-toned mixtures; in selecting a burnt sienna, the deepest or "mahogany" type will be found more useful than the paler, more opaque type. In a palette strictly limited to a very few colors, some painters employ it as a red, and it is sometimes classified as a red rather than as a brown.

The color effects of burnt sienna are illustrated in the frontispiece, which shows its characteristics in actual paint films: (D) when applied as an opaque or body-color; (E) as a transparent or glaze color; and (F) as a tinting color reduced with opaque white.

The umbers and burnt sienna have been in general use for a sufficient number of centuries to establish them as permanent and trustworthy pigments.

Burnt green earth or Verona brown is produced in some variety of shades, all quite intense, transparent, and valuable as glaze colors in oil painting. They are of lesser value, however, in techniques which require opaque effects, as they have very little hiding or tinting power. Burnt green earth is permanent in all techniques and, although not so well known and widely used as the other earth pigments, is a useful addition to the artist's palette.

Inferior and obsolete brown pigments

Vandyke brown, no longer in general use, is an earth containing undecomposed or partially decomposed vegetal matter. Oil paintings on which it has been used almost invariably turn dark and crack badly, although a few of the highest grades are permanent to light. Its popularity during the nineteenth century was due to the clear and deep tones it produces in mixtures of dark colors.

Sepia, obtained from the ink sacs of the cuttlefish, octopus, and other cephalopods, has been known and used as an ink and water-color brown since Roman times. On exposure to daylight it fades too badly to make it acceptable as an artist's pigment.

Bistre, obtained from the tarry mass resulting from incompletely burned beechwood, has properties and defects similar to those of sepia. The hue of sepia is approximated by burnt umber; that of bistre by raw umber.

Asphaltum, or bitumen, is not a true pigment, but a resinous or pitchy substance soluble in oils, yielding a blackish brown mass which is opaque when applied thickly and a transparent brown when applied thinly.

No longer in general use as an artist's pigment, asphaltum was one of the most destructive materials ever introduced into oil painting. Paintings in which it was employed—whether as a solid film, as a tinting color, or as a glaze—have invariably turned dark and cracked in wide open seams or fissures. Dug from deposits in the earth, it has been valued as a preservative or waterproofing material since prehistoric times. The blemishes and defects which develop on its surface with age, and which are ruinous to artists' paintings, do not affect its high performance in its other uses.

Mummy, supposedly an improved quality, was simply asphaltum recovered from Egyptian tombs.

Violet pigments

Cobalt violet. A furnace product, permanent for all uses, except that some samples are not limeproof and must be tested in lime plaster for six months before being used in fresco. It must also be excluded from pastels and from children's paints, because it is poisonous (it contains arsenic); but, in oil paints and in adults' water colors, it is a useful, bright, clear pigment.

Manganese violet. A duller and somewhat less satisfactory pigment than cobalt violet, but permanent for all easel painting techniques and not poisonous.

Mars violet. A pure iron oxide of the Indian red type, but much more bluish in mass-tone and in undertone; permanent, and suitable for all painting techniques. Compared with the brilliant cobalt and manganese violets, it is dull and muddy, but in many instances it is useful for violet and lavender effects.

Black pigments

Ivory black. This is the principal black pigment used by artists in all techniques. Originally made by burning ivory scraps, now made by carbonizing selected bones, it is superior to the ordinary bone black because it is made with greatest care from the best materials.

Lampblack and carbon black, made from the soot of burning petroleum products, are also permanent forms of pure or nearly pure carbon and can be used, but they are not so well adapted to artists' needs. They are extremely lightweight, fluffy powders; lampblack has a greasy nature, and carbon black—the most intense, jet-black of all—mixes poorly with other colors, its streaks persisting after much stirring and rubbing.

Drop black, vine black, and other varieties of carbon made by burning vegetal materials, are also permanent forms of carbon, but they are inferior in color and pigment properties to the best ivory black.

Mars black is an artificially produced form of iron oxide; unlike the other blacks, which are lightweight, fluffy, water-repellent powders composed of pure or nearly pure carbon, it is a heavy, dense material of the same physical or pigment properties as the other Mars colors. Although it has a rather reddish cast when compared with the more intense jet-black carbon pigments, most artists find it entirely satisfactory for all uses and some prefer it to the carbon blacks, especially in the water mediums. At present it is not made into paints by very many artists' material firms, but it is readily available in dry color form.

Mixed pigments

Most of the tube paints which contain a mixture of pigments but which are labeled with a single name, such as "Hooker's green," contain impermanent or doubtful materials and have been discarded or relegated to the status of obsolete or inferior colors. Some manufacturers put out colors, such as mixed or blended whites; others label colors with such unstandardized names as "Permanent green" which have never been officially accepted in any system of pigment nomenclature. Careful painters will not accept such vaguely described materials unless the maker also indicates the exact components on the label or in his literature.

Payne's gray. This is one of the few mixed pigments regularly accepted as permanent, if offered by a reliable maker. It is supposed to contain ultramarine blue, black and ochre. Most mixed colors are rejected by the experienced artist as unnecessary, because they increase the number of tubes of paint he must harbor and because he can easily mix the desired shades himself. However many painters consider Payne's gray an exception to this, because of the convenience in having this particularly useful combination on hand in ready-mixed form. This applies especially to water color, where it seems to fill a gap in the list of colors, and to be such a useful addition to the palette that it has survived for more than a century—long after similar mixtures have been abandoned.

Inert pigments

Inert pigments constitute a group of powders which are white or nearly white in the dry state; but, when ground in oil, they have little or no opacity and will impart no color effect to the chromatic pigments other than to detract somewhat from their clarity. Some of them retain their whiteness, however, in water mediums. The tinting strength of pigments or prepared artists' colors which contain appreciable amounts of such fillers or extenders will obviously be greatly weakened.

The pigment properties of the inert pigments and the qualities they will impart to paints vary considerably. Some of them are not just cheap extenders but are valuable and useful materials for certain purposes; as such they are used more often in industrial products than in artists' paints. The following are some of the more common inert pigments.

Alumina hydrate (aluminum hydroxide). A light, fluffy, pure white powder which becomes transparent and nearly colorless when ground in oil. Although a very slow drier in oil, it imparts excellent brushing qualities and desirable smoothness to colors and can be used as an extender in students' grade and other cheap colors. It is the principal *base* or inert pigment used in making clear, transparent lakes; the alizarin and madder reds contain it.

Blanc fixe (precipitated barium sulphate). A very dense, fine white powder used as a base for opaque lakes, as an extender or filler, and as a reinforcing or strengthening pigment in house paints. Native barium sulphate (barytes) is an exceptionally heavy material used only as a loader or cheapener of paints. Blanc fixe and alumina hydrate are the highest grade inert materials used to reduce the strength of pigments.

Chalk. Known in its purest form as precipitated chalk, this inert pigment is artificially manufactured and is used in several artists' materials such as gesso grounds, pastels, water paints, etc. In the dry state, it is a pure, snow-white, smooth powder which retains its whiteness in water mixtures but becomes muddy and yellowish when mixed with oil. Chalk has a high "bulking value" and contributes bulk or volume to paints. It is widely available in a standard U.S.P. grade at supply houses and drug stores and, although more expensive than whiting, is still of sufficiently low cost for large-scale use.

Whiting. Whiting is native or natural chalk, mined, ground, washed, and refined. Many industrial grades exist, but the average retail buyer at the paint stores is generally limited to the grade called "Extra Gilder's"; this is adequate for paint and gesso use but inferior in whiteness and uniformity to precipitated chalk, whose general properties it shares. When mixed with raw linseed oil, whiting forms the familiar putty, commonly used as a window cement, etc.

Silica or silex (powdered quartz). This is made in a variety of grades depending on its degree of coarseness and is used in some paints and grounds to impart roughness or "tooth" to surfaces, because even the more finely powdered grades retain their sharpness of particle form and produce this result in coatings.

Chapter 4

GROUNDS

Definition. The ground is the surface upon which an artist paints. In most painting techniques, a distinction is made between two elements, the *ground* itself, or the surface layer upon which the paint is applied, and the *support* or carrier of the ground; for example, linen or cotton canvas, wood or composition board or metal. Thus, the usual oil painting is executed on a ground made of two coats of white oil paint applied to a support which is a piece of linen cloth stretched on a wooden frame—the whole commonly referred to as a canvas.

Importance of grounds. From a purely artistic viewpoint, the ground on which an oil or tempera painting is executed or the wall which provides the background for a mural painting is just a blank area upon which the artist projects his ideas. For this reason, the ground and its support are likely to be considered as the elements furthest removed from the creative part of painting; in fact, in many instances they are taken for granted to such an extent that the considerations which govern their technical requirements are ignored or at least not given sufficient thought.

The permanence or durability of a painting, its optical or visual effect, and the excellence or successful execution of the artist's personal technique, all depend to quite a degree on the nature of the ground; therefore, far apart though it is from the artist's principal concern, these considerations are of extreme importance, and attention given to their correct preparation or selection will repay the painter in many ways.

58

Rule of gradation of layers. The ground is not merely a pleasant white surface applied to conceal the color of the support, but it is also a necessary and important part of the structure of a painting. A painting with its multiple layers of support, ground, coats of paint and varnish is a structure, and as such must conform with the age-old rules of construction which follow:

1. Never apply a brittle layer over a more flexible layer.
2. Never apply a layer containing strong binder over a weaker layer.

Disregarding the above precautions will invariably lead to cracking or disintegration of the coating. The opposite terms *brittle* and *flexible* are used in a relative sense, meaning simply that some layers or films will bend or stretch more readily than others.

3. Coarser layers should lie under finer layers; the first coat of a plaster, for example, always contains coarse ingredients, whereas the final coat is made up of more finely divided particles.
4. In thin coatings, layers of identical or nearly equal degree of strength, flexibility, and texture can ordinarily be used safely over each other.
5. Layers must have good or adequate adhesion or anchorage to each other. Roughness of texture (tooth), absorbency, or mutual cohesiveness is necessary to accomplish this. Any one of these conditions is normally sufficient to create good adhesion when the coating is acceptably strong, tough, and flexible. Ideally, all three should be present. The adhesion of paint to grounds is discussed on page 104.

GROUNDS FOR OIL PAINTING

Artists' canvas. Although the term canvas is sometimes applied to plain, coarsely woven cloth of vegetable origin, it is normally used among artists to denote a completely finished ground ready to paint on. Sometimes a completed oil painting is also referred to as a canvas, especially when someone is commenting on an artist's works.

Linen canvas. Strong, unbleached, pure linen is the standard material for an artist's canvas, and the best grades are woven especially for such purposes. A wide variety of weaves and weights is normally on the market; some of them are obtainable in very wide sizes for large paintings, but unfortunately the best grades of raw linen have never been very widely available to the retail purchaser since the demand for such a specialized item is comparatively small. Much of our artists' canvas is imported. Domestic canvas makers get most of their linen from Belgium and Ireland.

Cotton canvas. Cotton cloth is definitely inferior to linen for use in artists' canvases large or small and is employed only in cheap canvases or when linen is not available. Most prepared artists' canvas made of cotton is second-rate throughout. Cotton canvas stretches poorly, does not take the priming well, and is more susceptible to injury and to atmospheric changes than linen canvas. The textures imparted by cotton weaves are almost always less pleasing than those produced by linens. The primed cotton canvas of the shops can almost always be distinguished from good linen canvas by its slick, level finish, by its lack of boldness or character of weave and by its pale color and soft texture as compared with the tan color and harsher texture of linen.

Cotton-linen mixtures. Oil grounds *take* better on mixed weaves than they do on straight cotton, but such canvases have the serious fault of unequal tension. The two separate materials are affected differently by atmosphere and stretching; thus the ground is subject to surface inequalities and its use is avoided by careful painters.

Jute, burlap and similar coarse vegetal fibers are entirely unsuitable for permanent painting; they become extremely weak and brittle on short aging and are never used by conscientious painters.

Artists' canvas should be made of strong, stout material. The flimsiness and openness of weave of some of the cloth used at present, and in the recent past, are the direct causes of many failures such as cracking and flaking of the paint and ground, because of the inability of such canvas to withstand mild, mechanical shocks and wear. The most desirable weave is a close, square one in which the threads of the warp and filling are identical or equal.

All vegetal textile fabrics are harmfully affected when they are impregnated with oils; they rot, and become brittle and powdery with age. This action is prevented or minimized by sizing the cloth with a weak glue or gelatin solution before coating it with oil paint.

The terms "single-primed" and "double-primed" canvas as used by the canvas makers simply mean that the canvas has received either one or two coats of oil paint; double-primed canvas is the standard, and few, if any, experts recommend the use of a one-coat ground.

A nearly flawless, even weave is desired by most artists; irregular spots, knots or nubbles are likely to be most annoying. The fine, uniform flawless weave known as portrait linen is best for small works, and a more pronounced, bolder weave for larger paintings. Fine weaves are most suitable for precise, sharply painted styles, and coarse weaves for the heavier, more robust type of brush stroking.

The best-quality artists' canvas sold in the shops, ready for use, has been smoothly coated with two coats of oil paint. Because the cost of high-grade linen is such a large item, the maker will seldom skimp on these priming coats and so the primings found on good, stout linen are generally of high quality. On cotton canvas and on the cheaper grades of linen, however, the priming itself may also be inferior. Before purchasing canvas, the priming should be inspected closely and its adhesion to the linen tested by a vigorous bending and rolling of a small corner between the fingers. It should be remembered that any textile coating can be made to crack or break under such treatment, but a good indication of its quality can be obtained by observing the tenacity of the ground's adhesion to the linen and the manner in which the coating suffers. It should not dust or chalk away weakly; it should not be over-brittle and crack too easily. The average oil-painting canvas is semi-absorbent, made to suit the average straight oil-painting technique.

Prepared canvas is often grayish or yellowish; for optical reasons, as previously explained, the whitest kind is most satisfactory. Therefore, if it is desired for any reason to use a colored ground, better results are obtained when a glaze or veil of color is put over a white ground than when colors are mixed into the ground itself. However, no structural or chemical disadvantage occurs when the priming is tinted by mixing colored paints with it.

Making oil canvases. Sometimes an artist finds that it is desirable or necessary to make his own canvas. For this purpose, a piece of linen, preferably of a closely woven, even-textured material, is stretched so that the threads run parallel to the stretcher bars, and the surface is given a thorough coating of *weak* glue size as described on pages 75–77.

First priming. When the linen is dry it is restretched tightly if necessary and given a thin, uniform coating of white lead in oil,* thinned down with turpentine or mineral spirit to a consistency which allows an even coating. The proportion is two or three fluid ounces of turpentine to each pound of white lead in oil, varying somewhat according to circumstances. The consistency is not that of a conventional free-flowing or fluid paint, but the mixture is soft enough to be brushed out and distributed evenly. Too much turpentine yields a weak or insufficient coating; too little produces a film that is too glossy or too nonabsorbent for the average painting technique. A flat varnishing brush is most convenient for applying grounds.

---

* White lead in oil is sold in paint stores. It comes in one, five, twenty-five and hundred-pound containers; the best kinds bear the names of well-known, nationally distributed brands and have the contents on the labels—90 to 91 per cent basic lead carbonate plus 9 to 10 per cent raw linseed oil.

Second priming. After a day or two, the surface of the cloth, although still tender, will be dry enough to receive the second and final coat. Before applying it, the surface is tried by passing the palm of the hand lightly over it, and if there is any fuzz or hairy roughness, it is removed by a *very light* sandpapering, the sandpaper held loosely in the fingers, just so as to shave away the fuzz without grinding away the coating. The second coat is applied in the same way as the first, the priming being exactly the same as that of the first coat. It may contain slightly less turpentine but never any more than the first coat, as that would be likely to produce a somewhat less flexible layer which would be contrary to the rule forbiding application of a coat of paint over a more flexible coat. This kind of ground may be used as soon as it is completely hard and firm, which should be in about two weeks.

Effect of daylight. Grounds made of this type of industrial white lead in oil, require exposure to daylight for about ten days during the initial period of drying in order to prevent their turning yellowish. Should this occur, several days' exposure to daylight will restore them to their original creamy whiteness again. The raw linseed oil and the grinding methods employed in the manufacture of commercial white lead in oil make this product more susceptible to the presence and absence of light than the finer quality artists' flake or Cremnitz white oil paints.

Other white pigments as oil grounds. Zinc white, titanium white, lithopone, and mixtures of these materials have been used as grounds for oil canvases because purer or more brilliant white coatings can be produced with them than with straight white lead in oil, which by comparison produces rather creamy whites. Because of the inferior film or structural properties which these pigments impart to coatings, as compared with the good characteristics of a white lead in oil film, they are not recommended for home-made canvases. Commercial makers of artists' canvas, who have many more grades of materials and means of manufacture than are available to retail consumers, sometimes achieve good results with mixtures of these materials, but the straight white lead-in-oil ground as used for centuries is still the standard. The properties of these other pigments have been described under *White pigments.* The value of mixtures of white lead and zinc or titanium whites has been proved largely in house paints, which are ordinarily painted on rigid surfaces such as wood rather than on canvas. Since satisfactory grades of ready-prepared zinc and titanium whites of the same degree of quality and suitability as white lead are not ordinarily available in retail paint stores, the more expensive artists' material must be used when zinc or titanium is introduced into home-made grounds.

Utilization of old canvases. From the standpoint of permanence of effects and structural permanence, there are so many bad results when an oil painting is done over a completed old canvas that none of the makeshift methods of utilizing old paintings can be recommended. For temporary sketch or students' purposes, the old paint can be scraped or sandpapered down to an acceptable smoothness and given a coat of flat-white oil paint such as is sold for painting interior walls. Panels can be salvaged for professional use by sandpapering down the entire coating. The linen of a canvas can sometimes be salvaged, if it is of good, stout quality, by removing it from the stretchers and soaking it in a tub of water; this may, in many cases, make the entire paint and oil ground easily detachable from the cloth by dissolving the glue size. Few important, successful paintings of past art periods have come down to us on reused canvases, and the practice always leads to disagreeable or diastrous blemishes. There are some more remarks on this subject in relation to painting with oil colors, on page 116.

Stretching canvas. Tacking the canvas to a stretcher frame is not a difficult task, but unless one learns to do it *systematically* the results may be erratic. The important points are to make sure that

(1) The stretcher strips are assembled tightly and the corners are true right angles.

(2) The weave of the canvas is exactly parallel to the frame.

(3) The tacks are placed at regular intervals.

(4) The pull or tension used with the stretching pliers is uniform at each tack. Otherwise the canvas may very likely have the following faults:

> (1) Distortion of its rectangular shape so that it might not fit a picture frame.
>
> (2) Distortion and irregularity of weave.
>
> (3) Lack of tautness resulting in wrinkly or slack spots.
>
> (4) Bad warping of the frame from unequal tension, especially in the larger sizes.

A good system is to cut a piece of canvas with a margin all around about $2\frac{1}{2}$ inches more than the exact size. Then lay it face down on a table and place the assembled stretcher frame upon it, lining it up so that everywhere the weave is exactly parallel to the frame. Fold the canvas back over the edge of one side and drive in a tack at the middle of the strip. Number 3 or number 4 carpet tacks are generally used. Grip the edge of the canvas in the middle of the opposite stretcher strip at a point directly across from the first tack, see that the pliers are held snugly against the wood, draw the canvas taut with a moderately strong pull, and drive in the second tack. Repeat with the two other sides, being careful to maintain the parallel alignment of the weave. Do not drive in these first four tacks too securely at first, because it may be necessary to remove them again while adjusting the weave of the canvas. A medium-sized screwdriver is a handy implement for prying out tacks when necessary.

Now drive in a tack on each side of the first four tacks, using the same moderately strong pull and placing the tacks at regular intervals, say about two inches apart. Next, drive in the remaining tacks in the same way, working toward the corners and turning the canvas over to another side from time to time so that the over-all tension is kept equal. Do not tack the corners until all the remaining tacks are in place. To do the corners, face the rear of the canvas, and start by stretching and tacking

Fig. 7. Stretching the corners. Left end of strip.

Fig. 8. Stretching the corners. Right end of strip.

the left-hand end near the *front* edge (Figure 7); next, the right-hand end at the same corner by first folding the corner of the canvas and tucking it *in* neatly (Figure 8). Then with the aid of the stretching pliers drive in the tacks near the *rear* edge. The reason for these left-hand-front edge and right-hand-rear edge

FIG. 9. Stretcher keys.

instructions and for always tucking the canvas in over the right-hand ends will be seen immediately on examining the construction of a stretcher strip at these points: the idea is to drive the tacks into the center of the widest portion of the wood; this is always toward the front edge or face of the canvas at the left-hand end of each strip and toward the rear edge at the right-hand end. The little triangular wooden wedges or keys are lightly hammered into the slots two in each corner, after all the tacks are in. Normally they should not be forced in very far because the keys are intended to take up any subsequent slack by spreading the mitred corners away from each other, and they are best held in reserve to impart a final degree of taut-

Fig. 10. Special heavy stretcher.

ness to the canvas when required. Small brads hammered into edges of the stretcher strips at their ends will keep them from falling out (Figure 9).

Special extra-heavy, rigid stretchers with two crossbars are made to order by the firms which manufacture the regular stock strips (Figure 10). These can be ordered from any complete artists' supply shop, on reasonably short notice, and they can be made to any exact dimensions or with any desired number or arrangement of crossbars. Many careful artists prefer them, especially in large sizes, as they decrease the painting's fragility and its tendency to warp. These special strips are 2½ inches wide, are beveled on one side only, and their crossbars are keyed as well as their corners. Ordinary stretcher strips can also be ordered in fractional lengths or with crossbars.

PANELS

Wood panels. Wood panels have been used for easel paintings by European artists from the earliest days. They present a more rigid support for painting grounds than do canvases; they are therefore far superior for brittle and inflexible coatings, such as gesso, and they are also more satisfactory than woven textiles when smooth, textureless surfaces are preferred.

Wood panels, however, suffer from as many defects and ills as do linen canvases and, judging from the practical test of time, it cannot be said that one is more permanent than the other; in general, old oil paintings on canvas have survived in good condition as often as those painted on wood. Wood panels are subject to warping, cracking, and rotting, more rapidly in some climates than in others.

Wood panels may be classified in two types: (1) solid wood and (2) plywood, which is composed of relatively thin laminations or layers of wood glued together under pressure. Solid wood panels are principally of historical interest, because for many years the finest woodwork of all kinds has employed plywood or veneer, which is even more durable for paintings than panels made from one piece of wood. The early Italian easel paintings were largely done on very thick solid panels; the typical or usual wood employed was poplar. The Northern schools preferred thinner panels as a rule, and the wood was usually solid oak or mahogany.

Plywoods. The results of years of experience, corroborated by scientifically controlled tests, now show that a plywood or veneered wood panel is far less subject than a solid panel of equivalent dimension to cracking, warping, splitting, and other forms of decay. The following commercially available standard stock varieties are in use:

Five-ply maple, $1\frac{3}{16}$ inch thick; all five plies of equal thickness. This kind is made for technical use rather than for furniture purposes.

Five-ply birch or maple, $1\frac{3}{16}$ inch; the inner core is the thickest and is made of softer wood such as gum, and the two outer plies on each side are thin.

Five-ply maple, birch, walnut, or mahogany approximately $\frac{1}{4}$ inch thick; this type is less desirable than the heavier ones, especially in larger sizes.

The four above-named species of wood are believed to be of equal value, and no superiority of one over another has been established. Birch and maple, said to be least sensitive of the durable hardwoods to moisture, are likely to be the most available and least expensive. Panels with one-piece faces or the least number of joins are preferable.

Fig. 11. Sandpapering Presdwood.

Presdwood. One of the best materials to use as a support for painting grounds is a dense, compact wallboard known as *Presdwood.* This material is made by the Masonite Company of Chicago, and is composed of wood fibers united under great pressure. It contains no added binding materials, does not crack, split, or warp and has great durability. The other products of the same company, known as *Tempered Presdwood, Quartrboard,* and *Masonite* insulating board, are not recommended as they do not have the same good properties as the regular or un-tempered Presdwood.

Presdwood, ⅛ or ³⁄₁₆ inch thick, should be rubbed with very fine sandpaper until a fuzz is raised (Figure 11), then scrubbed with a cloth dipped in a mixture of three parts of denatured alcohol to one of clear ammonia. After this has evaporated, a gesso or oil ground is applied as later outlined in this chapter. The rough side of the panel could also be used without any further preparation, but the finish it produces is seldom liked by artists.

Presdwood has the advantage over wood panels in that it will not warp, crack or split under the average American climatic and housing conditions. Pieces larger than 24 inches, however, will curve and bend of their own weight, particularly when stored on edge. They should be braced by gluing or by employing a carpenter to glue a wooden frame or cradle to the back with strong casein glue or hot glue, using strong clamps while the glue is setting. The frames should be well joined at the corners and, depending on the size, should have crossbars (see Figure 12). The wood should be well seasoned, and strips approximately ¾ inch thick and 1¾ inches wide are most convenient. Some careful painters have all their panels cradled in this manner, down to the smallest sizes. In order to compensate for the pull of the coating, which may cause unbraced panels to curve, the backs should receive a thick coat of gesso or any kind of paint. Unbraced or unframed panels should be stored in a flat position rather than on edge.

Other wallboards. Several cheaper and less durable kinds of wallboard, such as the Beaver Board or Upson Board type and many others, are suitable for preparing panels for student's work and for temporary purposes. They should never be used, however, for permanent painting as they are not durable

FIG. 12. Rear of a cradled wallboard panel.

enough to resist the decay of aging or the wear of handling. Other hard, compact boards, similar in appearance to Presdwood, are on the market, but at present they are rather unknown items, as none have undergone the same period of trial and observation by artists.

Some artist painters have been rather dubious on the subject of the permanence of the adhesion of paint or glue coatings on Presdwood because it is a relatively new material and lacks the test of time that wood and linen have undergone. When applying either oil or gesso grounds to Presdwood panels, some cautious painters, following the old procedure for linen and wooden supports, apply a coat of thin, hot glue size as recommended for these supports on page 76. However, careful tests for adhesion and ease of coating with either oil or gesso grounds indicate that this is not entirely necessary. Figure 13 illustrates the adhesion of the gesso glue to unprepared Presdwood; on

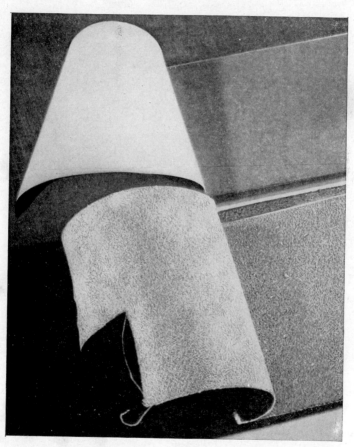

FIG. 13. Adhesion test, cloth glued to Presdwood with rabbit-skin glue. Above: On panel coated with oil paint. Below: On uncoated, smooth Presdwood. Test made by Julian Lamar.

the lower panel, a piece of fine linen was attached with a solution of rabbitskin glue. When this is pulled away from the surface by force, a whole layer of Presdwood fibers comes away with it, showing complete and efficient adhesion; on the upper panel the same test was repeated on Presdwood which had been given a thin coat of oil paint. Here the linen pulls off very easily and cleanly, indicating a superficial and probably impermanent adhesion.

Oil grounds on panels. Panels may be prepared with white lead in oil in much the same manner as canvas. When the panel is not abnormally or unevenly absorbent, the glue size may be omitted. It is customary to roughen the surface of the panel with sandpaper before applying the first coat. For very smooth surfaces the ground may be sandpapered with very fine abrasive paper. In order to produce a surface that has a coarse texture or tooth, powdered pumice or silica may be stirred into the final coating.

Metal grounds. In former times copper sheets have been used as supports for small paintings, but the practice never achieved much success; lack of adhesion and the development of blistering and flaking of the coating are common in these old works. The use of stainless steel and aluminum sheets is a modern development, which shows much promise but until there has been further research and standardization of artists' grounds on metals, they must be considered experimental.

The vast experience in applying coatings on aluminum gained in recent years, especially by the airplane industry, has shown that the production of durable grounds with permanent anchorage to this metal is by no means the simple procedure that was supposed when aluminum sheets first came into use. The natural oxide which forms on aluminum surfaces does not supply a good bond; aluminum panels require an electrolytic treatment and a corrosion-inhibiting primer before the ground or finishing coating is applied.

GLUES

Glues are used for the following purposes:

1. As an adhesive to join various materials such as wood, canvases, etc.
2. As a size or sealer for porous surfaces.
3. As a binder for some types of grounds (gesso).
4. As a binder or vehicle for coarse or cheap paints (poster colors, scenic colors, etc.).

The best glues are those made from the hides or skins of animals; the more delicate and tender the skin, the better the glue. The European craftsmen in Medieval and Renaissance times prepared a home-made glue by boiling parchment scraps and clippings, for which the modern equivalent is a very high-grade glue made from rabbit skins. Some of the finer calfskin glues are also useful. French rabbitskin glue comes in sheets about 7 inches square. (Figure 14).

Fig. 14. French rabbitskin glue.

Bone glue, fish glue, and other types are seldom desirable. Gelatin (Figure 15) is a highly purified material made from the same sources as the hide glues and is used to a limited extent in painting techniques, mainly as a sizing material rather than as a binder and adhesive.

A well-balanced glue has both high adhesive strength and high viscosity or jelling power; the rabbitskin and calfskin glues fill these requirements, but gelatin is second choice because it is not so good as a binder or adhesive, although it is an excellent sizing material. The most powerful glues are also the cleanest and purest and will produce the best results in every respect.

What a size is. A fluid material used as a size is distinctly different from a binder or an adhesive or a film-forming material. A size is employed to fill up pores in a porous surface, to render a surface less absorbent to subsequent applications of paints, etc., and to isolate the fibers of a material from the action of some other material. When a weak glue solution or a weak shellac solution is recommended as a size, it is intended to accomplish one of these purposes without forming a definite

FIG. 15. Sheets of gelatin.

or appreciable layer or skin after it has dried. If the solution is too strong or is applied too thickly, the result will not be that of a size; rather, it is likely to form a continuous layer or film, thus adding an element to the structure of the coating which is almost always undesirable. In the case of the weak glue or gelatin size recommended for linen, a thick layer is to be avoided as it would be a weak element in the structure of the canvas. It is very important to observe this precaution: to avoid, whenever a size is required, the formation of a continuous film of any appreciable thickness.

Approximately 1½ ounces of rabbitskin glue dissolved in a

quart of water (in the manner described on page 79) will yield
a size of the proper strength for treating linen canvas prior to
priming with oil paint. When cool, this solution should not
solidify at normal room temperature beyond the point of the
weakest sort of semi-jelly, as shown in Figure 16.

Fig. 16. Consistency of average glue-size cooled to room temperature.

Gesso Grounds *

The word "gesso" means a coating composed of chalk and
glue (or a modification thereof) and applied to a surface in

* Gesso and the preparation of gesso panels are gone into in such detail here
not because the subject is of greater significance than the others, but because
the material is more often prepared by the artist than it is purchased ready-
made, and also because it demonstrates a set of instructions typical of the kind
of procedure an artist is called upon to perform when he prepares his own
materials.

order to produce a smooth, level white surface for decoration with paint, gilding, etc.

The term is taken from the Italian, dating at least as far back as the fourteenth century. Cennino Cennini * and other early writers made a distinction between two materials: *gesso sottile* or finishing gesso which was equivalent to the chalk-glue mixture described here and *gesso grosso* which was a coarser material formerly used as an underlayer in building up foundations, especially on heavily ornamented carved surfaces such as frames, furniture and the like, but probably not on fine, flat surfaces. Its composition was sometimes plain, raw plaster of Paris, glue solution mixed with raw plaster, or a mixture of plaster with some *gesso sottile*.

Gesso and its application are simple, and perfect results are easy to obtain; complicating the simple instructions merely leads to complications in results. If the glue is too weak, the gesso will be too soft; if the glue is too strong, the gesso will be too hard and likely will crack. Cracking also occurs when a stronger gesso is applied over a weaker layer, and sometimes when the panels are made in a damp or unheated room. Pin-holes are caused mostly by air bubbles or foamy gesso; they appear most frequently when the gesso is too weak, and when the underlayers were too dry. The defects of *simple* gesso show up immediately upon the complete drying out of the surface, and if the gesso surface is good at that time it is almost certain to remain so indefinitely.

The average gesso surface for modern use should be hard and strong; it should not be too easy to dent, scratch or chip off with the thumbnail, but it should not be so hard that it will present too much difficulty in the smoothing or finishing operations.

Composition of gesso. The classic recipe for gesso as recorded by Cennino Cennini employs parchment glue and an inert white powder (calcium sulphate) made by slaking plaster of Paris. Precipitated chalk or a fine grade of purified whiting (these white powders have been described under **Inert Pig-**

* See page 141.

ments) soon came into use, as improved or more available replacements became obtainable. Modern gesso is made of a solution of rabbit- or calfskin glue and chalk. The best modern gesso recipes do not differ appreciably from the earliest ones and, although some care and skill are necessary to make good gesso panels, ability to prepare them is quickly acquired without too much trouble.

Typical recipe for gesso for panels. Soak 3 ounces of French rabbitskin glue in 28 fluid ounces of cold water over-

Fig. 17. Left: French rabbitskin glue soaked in water for 36 hours. Right: Same glue before soaking.

night, or until it has swollen and absorbed its full capacity of water. It should then be of a uniform pale color and of soft consistency throughout, without any dark or tough spots (Figure 17). If the glue comes in large sheets it should first be wrapped in a cloth and broken into small pieces.

Place in a double boiler and heat, with occasional stirring, until dissolved. No glue solutions should ever be boiled, overheated or scorched as this would immediately throw off their properties in an erratic manner and destroy all accuracy and control of recipes; that is why a double boiler is necessary. Pour the glue into a quart measure and add the few ounces of water necessary to bring its volume up to one quart. Replace in the double boiler, heat thoroughly, and it is ready for use.

FIG. 18. Thin cream consistency of gesso for brushing.

The hot glue solution is mixed with precipitated chalk to a *thin* cream consistency as demonstrated in Figure 18. Water and glue are measured accurately and the consistency is varied according to the amount of chalk added; about a pound or a little less to a quart of glue solution is average. It is customary to replace two ounces or so with zinc or titanium white in order to increase opacity. If, instead of being used, the glue were allowed to cool in the pot overnight at normal room temperature it would set to a jelly, as illustrated in Figure 19. One way to test the glue for strength is by an inspection of this jelly. When the smooth surface of the jelly in the pot is parted with the fingers, it should break as it does in the illustration, a rather clean break at the surface and a rough granular break through its mass. A clean, sharp break all the way down shows it to be too strong, whereas a soft, ragged break on the surface indicates that it is too weak.

Supports for gesso grounds. Gesso is usually applied to rigid panels of wood or a durable wallboard, such as Presdwood (see page 71), by brushing on the liquid gesso in several coats as uniformly and evenly as possible. When the coating is dry, the brushmarks are rubbed down so that the surface is smooth and flawless. Gesso is not well adapted for coating canvas. The cloth is too flexible and too susceptible to the action of atmospheric moisture from the rear to be considered safely permanent. When special precautions are observed, a fairly durable but

FIG. 19. Consistency of gesso glue cooled to room temperature.

very thin ground is sometimes made on canvas—especially on the reverse side of a prepared oil canvas where the oil priming acts as a stiffener or reinforcement as well as a moisture resister —but, in general, this practice is not to be recommended. Canvas is of principal value as a support for oil grounds. If a canvas or canvas-like texture is preferred to the standard ivory-smooth gesso finish, it can be obtained either by gluing coarse linen on the panel before applying the gesso or by impressing the weave of cloth on the final coating of gesso while it is drying, at the moment when it is dry enough to resist being picked up and, at the same time, soft enough to receive the impression.

FIG. 20. Gesso panel: Brushing the first coat.

Before applying gesso, the panels must be prepared in accordance with the instructions mentioned at the end of the section on wallboard panels on page 71.

Application of gesso. The gesso must be applied in several thin layers or coats, and in order to insure uniformity of the whole coating, it is important to use liquid gesso of the same strength throughout the application. It is also important to remember that glue gesso must be at the same uniform heat when its consistency is judged. Some careful workers will use a thermometer to maintain a constant temperature, but with a little experience this should not be necessary as there is some leeway. The first coat should be applied as hot as possible, and manipulations will be easier in subsequent coats if the liquid is kept warm, but continual heating in the double boiler while in use, sometimes causes pinholes to form. The cooler the glue mixture, the thicker and less brushable will be the coatings.

FIG. 21. Gesso panel: Removal of air-bubbles in first coat by stroking with fingertips.

Enough gesso must be put on the panel so that the final dried coating may be sandpapered to a smooth finish, free from the rather heavy brushmarks which are normally present, without the sandpaper going through and exposing the panel at any point. This will take four or more coats.

First coat. After brushing the first coat onto the panel (Figure 20), any air bubbles are smoothed away with the fingertips (Figure 21). This results in a rather thin and not very opaque layer. Any roughness of fingermarks will be concealed by the next coat and can be disregarded.

Subsequent coats. Each coat is applied as soon as the previous coat is dry enough to withstand it and not be picked up by the

Fig. 22. Gesso panel: applying a coating.

Fig. 23. Gesso panel: Smoothing out a coating.

brushing. Each coat will take longer to dry than the preceding coat because of the greater moisture-retention of the built-up layers. The gesso is applied with a thin flat brush (a varnish brush or artists' extra-wide, flat, bristle brush is best). A full brush stroke is drawn rapidly across one edge of the panel, with a waggling wrist motion such as house painters use (Figure 22); then with straight, light strokes (Figure 23), it is

FIG. 24. Gesso panel: Removing brush-strokes with abrasive paper.

smoothed *in one direction only* until the brush begins to drag and the gesso begins its initial set; the brushing is stopped immediately at this point and the next stroke commenced.

The same brush stroke method is repeated on the rest of the coats, but each time the panel is turned so that the strokes are at right angles to those of the previous coat. This is most important if a level, smooth layer is to be produced.

Finishing the panels. At any time after the final coat has become thoroughly dry, the panels may be brought to a smooth, level surface by rubbing them down to remove brush marks and other irregularities. The most widely used method is to rub the surface with fine-grain abrasive paper (Figure 24), several varieties of which are useful. The 4/0 grain (150) is usually considered best, as it will take down the irregularities of surface rapidly enough and not scar the finish too deeply. A still finer

FIG. 25. Gesso panel: The use of the sandpaper block.

FIG. 26. Gesso panel: The wet cloth method of polishing.

grain is preferred by some. Garnet paper and some of the synthetic aluminum oxide abrasives work well. Ordinary or common sandpapers are not satisfactory; they stain the surface and are not sharp enough for use on gesso of the required hardness. For a mechanically perfect, level surface a sandpaper block can be used (Figure 25).

Any fine abrasive scratches may be smoothed (or the entire finishing operation may be accomplished) by another method—rubbing with a soft cotton cloth dipped in water, well wrung out, and smoothly folded to a wad (Figure 26). This method dissolves a tiny surface layer and distributes it evenly over the surface.

A third means of producing a smooth surface is to use a soaking wet block or lump of pumice which has been brought to a smooth flat surface by rubbing it on fine sandpaper. Experience and practice will develop a good technique, and personal preferences for these various methods of smoothing gesso panels will be established. If powdered pumice is used in connection with a wet rubbing method, sufficient pumice will remain embedded in the surface after drying to produce a finish with a considerable degree of tooth.

Defects of gesso panels

Pinholes may be caused by careless application, air bubbles (especially in the first coat), the preceding coat being too dry, or the gesso being too foamy. In the panel illustrated (Figure 27) a narrow strip down the center has been sandpapered.

Paint will seldom conceal pinholes; as shown in Figure 28, thin layers of color will accentuate them.

Cracking (Figure 29) may occur if the glue is too strong or stronger than the preceding coats; if a single coat is too thick; or when the room is cold and damp. Cracks occurring long after the panel is finished are usually the fault of the support.

Preparation for painting. A gesso panel may be, and ordinarily is, painted on directly, without further preparation, when tempera, water-color or gouache paints are used. For normal oil painting, it is necessary to reduce its absorbency or porosity by sizing lightly with very much thinned-out shellac or a very dilute gelatin solution; this will cut down (but not eliminate entirely) the absorbency of the surface so that painting manipulations may be properly carried out. The reasons

FIG. 27.

for desiring this condition are discussed on pages 104 and 105. If too much size is applied the panel will become so nonabsorbent that the painting will not take well nor have good anchorage to the surface. Some painters apply the size after an outline drawing, thus combining its function with that of a fixative for the drawing.

Casein gesso. Casein is a material from which adhesive and binder solutions can be made; its properties and the methods of handling it are described on page 157.

Some painters and some commercial firms have used casein in painting grounds, where it serves fairly well, but such grounds are distinctly second-rate compared to those made with glue.

Casein is a "cold glue"; that is, after making the solution, whether for adhesive, gesso or paint-binder use, it may be applied cold, whereas glue solutions must be kept at a fairly

FIG. 28.

high and uniform temperature during their use. In making grounds, this is its sole advantage. Casein gesso is more difficult to handle and apply than glue gesso; it is more readily subject to decay and defects; its texture and behavior toward paints are liked less by expert painters; it is also subject to increasing embrittlement on aging. When making gesso panels from casein mixtures, the procedures to be followed are the same as those given for glue gesso, except that the casein coating is used at room temperature. Because it can be applied cold it may also be used in spray guns.

Perhaps the greatest drawback to the use of casein in any home-made product is the difficulty of maintaining uniformity of binding strength, due not only to the variation in different

FIG. 29.

lots of the raw material, but also to the changes it undergoes on aging. A few months' storage will alter its properties erratically, so that a different formula must be used from the one employed on fresh material.

All in all, casein has proved more successful in the case of professional workers in shops where continuous processes and systematic controls are in operation than when used occasionally by artists.

Emulsion grounds. The use of grounds made with emulsion binders or part oil paint and part water-adhesive (casein, glue, egg, etc.) has little or no precedent beyond comparatively recent times, with the exception of a few obscure references to the addition of starch or flour to oils in some ancient manuscripts.

Most authorities do not favor such mixtures in grounds for permanent painting on canvas because they do not have sufficient qualites of flexbility, toughness, adhesion or resistance to moisture. Like gesso grounds and tempera paints they are best adapted for use on panels, but even there they are sometimes inferior to simple gesso grounds. They are relatively spongy and porous, which imparts to them a deceptive flexibility when fresh—the sort of flexibility a slice of fresh bread has—but they become very brittle with age. Casein and oil mixtures are especially bad in this respect; casein coatings embrittle with age, and all casein-oil mixtures eventually turn yellow.

Student and Sketching Panels

Oil ground. The ready-made canvas boards and academy boards which are sold for temporary sketch purposes are usually adequate but should not be used for permanent, serious works of art as their materials and workmanship are usually of an inferior nature. For larger sizes such panels are usually home-made, by applying two thin coats of ready-mixed, flat white oil paint, such as is available for interior house use, to Presdwood panels. Lighter weight and cheaper panels can be made by using common wallboard (Beaver Board, Upson Board, etc.) instead of Presdwood. When a less absorbent coating is required, the panel is sized with a thin coat of shellac before applying the paint. A coat of any sort of paint or varnish on the back side will prevent excessive curving or warping of the board to some extent.

Gesso ground. Substitute gesso panels can be made by applying two or three coats of prepared casein wall paint to panels, using the same general methods of application and finishing as described under gesso. The brilliant white, simple casein paints sold in paste form in cans (Sunflex, Luminal, etc.) are preferable to the more recently "improved" resinous types (Ultra Luminal, Kem-tone, etc.). However, none of these products is recommended for professional artists' permanent painting.

Chapter 5

OIL PAINTING

Painting in oil is by far the most important and popular method of easel painting. As a method or technique, it has been completely and thoroughly studied and recorded from every viewpoint. This means that the present-day painter has at his command—if he is conscientious enough to learn and apply them—all the details necessary for successful manipulation of effects, as well as safeguards for the longevity of the painting and the variations for creating styles to suit individual requirements. The positive data we have concerning these matters have been gained from several different sources: from the records and examples of more than six centuries of European development; from the researches of scholars and scientists into past practices; from laboratory investigations, analyses and reconstructions; and from adapting results of similar modern research on the same materials, which is always being carried on by workers in related fields—for instance, scientific work on industrial paints.

Linseed oil. Linseed oil is expressed from the seed of flax plants. When used in paints it dries to form an adequately durable film which performs all four functions of a paint vehicle, as outlined on page 6. Linseed oil does not "dry" in the same sense as water, turpentine, or benzine. It is not volatile, and does not evaporate and disappear into the air; instead, when it is spread out in a thin layer and exposed to the air it jells and then hardens. After going through a series of chemical changes, it becomes converted to a new substance; if it has been properly combined with the right pigments, in the correct proportions, it forms an adequately tough, leathery, adherent film, resistant to solvents and capable of surviving for centuries on works of art. There are two principal chemical changes undergone by vegetable drying oils in their conversion from the fluid to the insoluble, solid form—absorption of oxygen from the air (oxidation) and an internal or structural change (polymerization) in which the molecules of the oil become rearranged.

There are, of course, numerous grades, varieties and degrees of refinement of linseed oil, and small differences or variations in the raw materials and processing methods will produce oils of extremely varying characteristics—something which is also true of other products refined or processed from vegetal sources. Some linseed oils, although excellent for the purposes for which they are produced, make poor artists' colors. Some specially refined linseed oils are useful in artists' mediums and are discussed further on in this chapter.

The best oil for artists' oil colors is called cold-pressed linseed oil. Clear pale amber or golden in color, it is pressed from the seeds without the aid of steam and purified by simple methods. Most linseed oils are pressed hot, and are then subjected to more complex treatments of refining, and they are for the most part inferior to the cold-pressed oil. This is especially true of those which have been bleached with acid to a pale straw color, as these revert, upon aging, to a dark or deep amber shade.

Other drying oils. Although not all vegetable oils are drying oils, about fifty can be expressed from various seeds, nuts, etc., and could be utilized as drying oils for one purpose or another. However, because of their shortcomings and defects, none of these has ever been used extensively in artists' paints, with the exception of poppy oil and walnut oil. Walnut oil has long been discarded from the lists of approved artists' materials because of its inferiority to linseed and poppy oils. Poppy oil is valuable as an ingredient to improve the smoothness of some linseed oil colors, but it is better not to use it in amounts greater than 25 per cent, preferably about 15 per cent. Poppy

oil alone forms a film which is weaker and less permanent than
linseed oil, it does not dry so well, and it cannot be used with
the same freedom or for the same number of varied purposes.
In its original state, poppy oil is much paler than raw or cold-
pressed linseed oil, but this advantage is outweighed by more
important disadvantages. Poppy oil is in second place to linseed oil as an ingredient of permanent paints, its chief use
being as an addition to linseed oil colors. It is never employed
as an ingredient of clear varnishes or glaze mediums, nor used
in complicated techniques. At the present time few brands of
artists' paints use poppy oil as the sole or principal paint vehicle. Colors ground in poppy oil can be distinguished from
linseed oil colors by their lack of odor, since linseed oil has a
characteristic smell.

Mᴀɴᴜғᴀᴄᴛᴜʀᴇ ᴏғ Aʀᴛɪsᴛs' Oɪʟ Cᴏʟᴏʀs

　　Modern dry pigments are put on the market in fine, uniform, powder form; care is usually taken to have the particle
size of each individual pigment correct, so that its color characteristics and its physical or mechanical behavior in paints
will conform to the highest standards. Consequently, the grinding of paints is necessary, not so much for making the pigment
particles smaller as for breaking up the lumps and producing
an intimate mixture in which each little particle or grain is
completely surrounded by the liquid vehicle. No mixture of
pigment and oil which has simply been stirred together or
lightly rubbed (as with a spatula or palette knife) is a paint;
it is merely a paste, which will contain a great excess of vehicle,
will be largely made up of microscopic clumps of semi-dry pigment, and will be full of air bubbles. A real paint, having
plastic qualities and which will flow and manipulate properly
and form a durable, permanent film when dry, must be ground
by *strong friction* in order to break up the little clumps and to
insure that the particles are completely wetted or surrounded
by the oil. The same is true of the water paints described in
following chapters.

The paint manufacturer stirs dry pigment and oil in a very powerful mechanical mixer until a smooth, stiff paste is obtained. The paste is then run through roller mills which grind it into paint, doing a much more efficient job than is possible by hand methods of grinding, and turning out a product that is seldom equaled by hand grinding.

FIG. 30. Oil paint; Mixing oil and pigment.

Home-made oil colors. The necessary equipment is simple: a strong, flexible but not too limber spatula or palette knife, a slab made of plate glass with a roughened or ground surface (some workers prefer a slab of marble or some harder stone), and a muller made of stone or glass. The grinding surface of the muller should have a roughened, ground glass finish and it should be not less than 2½ inches in diameter. The grain or tooth of the grinding surfaces of muller and slab can be produced or sharpened by grinding with an abrasive powder such as Carborundum mixed with water or turpentine. The slab can be of large size and permanently attached to the table top, or it can be as small as 12 inches square. It can be kept from

FIG. 31. Oil paint: Grinding with a glass muller.

shifting about during the grinding by strips of wood or molding, flush with its surface and nailed or screwed to the table along three or four sides.

The mulling of paints. In grinding paints, pigment and oil are first rubbed together with the spatula (Figure 30), using the smallest amount of oil to produce the stiffest workable paste. This paste, which is not yet a *paint* (because it does not have the required consistency or plasticity) is spread on the slab and ground thoroughly with the muller (Figure 31), until it is a smooth, glossy paint which is free from grittiness and specks of unground pigment. After about 25 to 50 rubs, the paste must be scraped from the slab and from the edges and bottom of the muller (Figure 32). It is gathered together and given another

FIG. 32. Oil paint: Gathering the paint from muller and slab.

25 to 50 rubs, and this procedure is continued until the entire batch is thoroughly and smoothly ground. If the grinding makes the paint too thin, more pigment is added and the grinding continued. There are other systems of handling the paste during grinding, but these instructions are typical.

Consistency of paint. All pigments do not react with oil in the same manner. Some, such as white lead, will produce very good paints, smooth and short (buttery); others, such as ultramarine, have a tendency to be long and stringy; still others, like cobalt yellow, are inclined to become grainy or crystalline. Artists can accommodate their painting manipulations to the various natural characteristics of the individual pigments, as was done to some extent in the past. However, today the manufacturer has learned from long experience how to turn out a whole set of colors all of which come out of their tubes in much the same consistency, with a close similarity of handling properties, and within a reasonably close range of drying speeds. The manufacturer gets these results by proper manipulation of mixing and grinding operations and by the addition of modifying ingredients. These added materials should be chosen from time-tested ingredients known not to be detrimental to the permanence of the finished painting. It is permissible to adjust the properties of paints with them provided that they are *not used in excessive amounts.*

Plasticizers. This term is applied to modifying ingredients which are added to paints in order to make them more controllable in manipulations and to increase or prolong their flexibility. It is also applied to materials used for the same purposes in all other mixtures and compounds, such as water paints, glues, lacquers, plastics, etc.

A much used and generally approved plasticizer and stabilizer for tube colors is white refined beeswax which aids in making the paint smoother, tends to prevent separating of the oil, and helps keep the dried paint film supple and flexible.

A wax-like, fluffy, lightweight powder called aluminum stearate is almost universally employed by commercial paint manufacturers to give a smooth consistency to the paint and as a stabilizer to keep pigment and oil from settling in the tubes during storage. Because use of this powder demands considerable knowledge and experience, and because so many types and varieties are employed, beeswax is preferred for amateur paint grinding. Provided the amount of stearate or wax is kept to a minimum, that is, no more than the small amount usually necessary to improve the consistency, it is not considered harmful.

The use of poppy oil as an addition to linseed oil colors has already been noted; if, instead of pure cold-pressed linseed oil, a mixture is used which contains four parts of cold-pressed linseed oil and one part of poppy oil, the consistency of those pigments which naturally tend to make stringy or sticky paint will be considerably improved.

Small amounts of water or of emulsions which contain water are generally condemned by all competent authorities for this purpose. Adding water is an easy way to stiffen and improve the consistency of some oil paints and also to preserve consistency in the tubes, but paints containing it will eventually harden in the tubes and their dried paint films will be likely to fail in several respects.

Adding too much of these modifying ingredients may lower a paint's quality in three ways:

1. By lessening its tinting strength, brilliance, clarity, or hiding power.
2. By causing rapid yellowing of the paint film
3. By decreasing its toughness or flexibility, thus leading to cracking or other failures.

Normal oil content of paints

There is sufficient oil in a well-made oil color to insure the permanence and durability of the paint film; in fact, it contains a surplus over the amount which is actually required to bind the pigment and anchor it to the ground. This surplus is necessary in order to grind the pigment to a smooth paste and to give the paint the right brushing properties.

Some pigments require a greater amount of oil than others in order to make a smooth plastic paint; the degree, in relation to the pigment's volume or weight, is called its "oil absorption." Naturally, most oil paints made with pigments which have a high oil absorption will yield rather flexible oil films, while those of low oil absorption will tend to give more brittle results. Thus it is of some importance for the painter to learn into which class the various pigments fall, if he is to avoid possible cracking of paint films through superimposing brittle coatings over flexible ones.* An exaggerated example would be a layer of zinc white over a solid coating of burnt umber—which would mean cracking within a very short time.

Excessive oil in paints. An excessive amount of oil beyond the normal surplus—sometimes found in poorly ground colors —or additional oil added to paint may cause after-yellowing and also wrinkling of the film. Obviously, then, it is important for the artist to use colors containing the lowest percentage of oil, with which smooth-working, well-ground paints can be made, and to refrain from adding linseed oil to paints except when it is a component of a well-balanced painting or glaze medium. Such mediums (page 107) are made with selected non-yellowing oils, and their varnish content prevents their weakening or softening the paint film. Excess oil which has separated from paint in the tube may be drained off by allowing the paint to stand for a few minutes on a sheet of writing paper; if the remainder of the paint is too stiff or over-pigmented to work well, it should be discarded. When paint becomes useless through hardening or "livering" in the tube, it means either that it was made of inferior materials poorly ground, or else that it contained too large an amount of drier or other modifying ingredient. Unlike hardened water colors which can be reworked, hardened oil paints cannot be reclaimed because the setting of a drying oil is not a reversible process.

Filling of tubes by hand. Home-made paints can be packed in pure tin tubes as shown in Figures 33 to 38 which follow.

---

* Oil absorption data may be studied in the author's *The Artist's Handbook*, Viking Press, New York, 1940.

FIG. 33. Filling. Cap was removed and then replaced after first portion had been settled down into neck of tube.

FIG. 34. To settle paint down into tube, fist is pounded on table. Tapping cap directly on table would crumple shoulder of tube.

FIG. 35. More than an inch must be left empty at the bottom.

FIG. 36. Bottom is pressed firmly with a strong spatula. Tube is raised
with finger and—

FIG. 37. Allowed to fall of its own weight. This folding is repeated once more.

FIG. 38. A final crimping with the stretching pliers adds security to the closure.

BASIC PRINCIPLES APPLIED TO OIL PAINTING

In Chapter 1 the nature of paint is described, and the basic principles or mechanics of painting are summarized on page 13. An oil painting must be considered as a structure. Therefore, just as a building, a highway, or a bridge must conform to age-old principles of engineering, so an oil painting must conform to long-established rules which govern the building-up of layers or coatings, superimposed one over the other. Since the ground, the paint layers, and the individual ingredients of these, all are elements of the whole painting, they must be built up in relation to each other and to the whole in order to obtain satisfactory results.

One of the most important of these rules is the previously mentioned (page 59) admonition never to paint coats over more flexible layers, or else cracking will occur. When painting on an oil canvas it should be remembered that the ground itself has some degree of flexibility, which limits the use of paints to those that are at least as flexible as the priming on the canvas.

Adhesion or anchorage of coatings. Paint (and for that matter gesso, oil grounds, plaster, and any other coating as well) must adhere permanently to the surfaces to which it is applied; flaking, peeling, blistering, and similar defects are most frequently caused by simple lack of adhesion. Aside from the adhesive or glue-like action of the coating itself, permanent adherence depends largely on the nature of the surface to which it is applied. There are two kinds of surfaces which are satisfactory for promoting and assisting permanent adherence of coatings.

1. An absorbent or porous surface which will partially imbibe the paint vehicle.
2. A rough, textural surface (granular, fibrous, web-like or scored) which will hold the dried paint in a mechanical grip or bond.

A slick, shiny completely nonabsorbent surface is the least likely to offer permanent adhesion. A coating which is too absorbent is generally not desirable; for example, an un-sized gesso coating with full absorbency may take water color and tempera very well, but it will absorb so much of the oil vehicle as to leave the paint in a weak condition, a development more likely with heavy, thick coatings than with thin or very thin coats. Extreme absorbency can be reduced by the use of size, as previously mentioned.

As a general rule, a combination of the proper degree of tooth plus the proper degree of absorbency is desirable. However, for some painting methods the coarseness of texture of a nonabsorbent ground or the absorbency of a smooth ground will alone suffice to promote good adhesion of the surface coating to the support.

Role of the ground in painting manipulations. The very same qualities which make for permanent *adhesion* between paint and ground or between layers of paint are also desirable for assisting the *manipulation* of paint in most oil-painting techniques. The worst surface on which to attempt manipulating oil paint would be a slick shiny one, such as a sheet of glass. Ordinary brush or painting-knife strokes could not be used with any control or precision, and the result would almost certainly be smeary and undesirable. If the surface has the proper degree of tooth (coarseness of grain) or roughness, or if it is somewhat absorbent, the color is taken from the brush in a satisfactory way and subsequent manipulations can be carried out well. On the other hand, if a surface is too fully absorbent and takes in too much of the oil vehicle, it may cause extreme difficulty in handling or manipulation and hamper free stroking since the brush becomes exhausted immediately.

The use of turpentine. In order to brush out oil paints and to spread them around or thin them so that they can be smoothly brushed out to thin layers—*and for no other reason*—

turpentine or mineral spirit * is added to the colors during the painting. Practice in painting is the only way to learn how much turpentine to use. Most painters work it in by occasionally dipping the brush in a small cup full of the thinner and mixing it with the paint on the palette. The object is to add just enough thinner to serve the purpose, but not to introduce so much into the paint that it becomes "runny" or that a weakened paint film results. Naturally, a thin layer of paint will dry more rapidly than a heavier coating; therefore a paint which contains a volatile solvent or diluent will dry faster, because its oil content is more exposed to the oxygen of the air. The paint will also *set up*; that is, it will assume a gelatinous rather than a fluid condition, as soon as the volatile portion of the vehicle evaporates. Other than by these mechanical aids, volatile diluents or thinners do not promote the drying action or the chemical hardening of oil.

There are numerous other volatile solvents having greater or lesser speed of evaporation and degree of solvent action, but turpentine and mineral spirit will serve almost every need of normal oil painting.

Mat and gloss finishes in oil painting. One of the striking features which appealed most strongly to the first generations of painters who used oily paint vehicles was the fact that full-toned glossy paintings could be more directly painted than was possible with the use of aqueous paints. For hundreds of years thereafter oil painting was supposed to be glossy; it was not until quite recent times that any attempts were made to imitate with it the lusterless finishes of fresco, water-color and gouache paints.

A normal oil painting is intended to have some degree of gloss; results of all the experience in technical work on indus-

* A petroleum solvent, made especially for paint use and sold in bulk in paint stores. Also called "turpentine substitute," or sold under trade names such as "Varnolene." As a paint thinner, a brush and palette cleaner, and an all-around studio solvent, its action is about the same as turpentine. It usually costs about one fifth as much as turpentine. It evaporates more slowly than the ordinary benzines or naphthas and is less dangerously inflammable.

trial coatings show a very definite inferiority in the permanence and longevity of coatings when they are made lusterless. Gloss can be dulled in several ways, such as by decreasing the percentage of binder or by adding waxes or other ingredients, all of which weaken the paint film, make it more susceptible to the development of defects, and lower its resistance to wear.

Reliance on excessive use of turpentine or on the absorption of paint by an overabsorbent ground is not only likely to produce a weak and faulty coating, but the paint quality so produced will generally be unsuccessful.

The best flattener for oil paintings would probably be the use of a reliable mat varnish which would produce an over-all, uniform dull finish and permit the retention of a full paint quality and a depth of color—but, unfortunately the mat varnishes on the market at the present time, leave much to be desired. They either contain materials which will turn yellow on short aging or have large percentages of wax (or waxy ingredients) which do not form a sufficiently durable coating to withstand normal wear; or else they will quickly polish to a glossy finish when rubbed. Waxes are among the most permanent and moisture-resistant of our materials and are useful ingredients of various painting materials, but they are not ideal additions to picture varnish. A wax paste—made by melting white refined beeswax, removing it from the stove and thinning it to the consistency of floor wax by stirring in some turpentine or mineral spirit—makes a fine preservative and finish for paintings *which have previously been varnished*.

PAINTING MEDIUMS

When more complex methods of oil painting are used, especially those which employ thin coats of paint, glazes (thin, transparent films of paint, applied over dried underpaintings) and the like, it sometimes becomes necessary to make the paint very thin and fluid. This is accomplished by using a liquid which not only dilutes the vehicle but also contains "fixed" or solid ingredients with film-forming properties in themselves.

These leave behind them, when dry, substances which reinforce or assist in the film-forming action of the original paint vehicle instead of evaporating completely like the volatile thinners. Such liquids are called painting mediums, or glaze mediums. A good definition of a paint medium, then, is a liquid which, when added to a fluid paint, will contribute desirable properties to its workability and also because of its film-forming or plasticizing ingredients, to the final paint coating. Ordinary oil painting of average thickness does not require the use of mediums.

There are many oil painting mediums in use by artists, the best of them being simple mixtures of time-tested ingredients which have been generally approved because of the permanent results observed over long periods of time. There are also some overcomplicated mixtures, as well as concoctions of undesirable ingredients. The harmful effects of many of these were known a long time ago, but their recipes occasionally survive or are revived from time to time and hailed as inventions. At the present writing there are no improved oil-painting mediums made with modern or recently developed ingredients.

Oil-painting mediums are usually mixtures of specially refined linseed oils and varnishes; they are generally prepared with turpentine or petroleum thinners, in thin, ready-to-use form. The mixture of oil and varnish is used rather than a single oil or varnish because the balance of properties (see page 7) makes it necessary for the medium to meet a number of requirements, and no single ingredient can comply with the various functions which a painting or glazing medium is called on to perform. Mediums must mix perfectly with oil paint; they must not alter the character of the painting too far from that of plain oil paint; they must allow easy manipulation, without flaws or blemishes; they must leave the final paint in the same permanent, durable state as though plain oil colors had been used.

Driers. Some mediums and oil paints require the addition of driers. The artist should look upon a drier as an occasionally necessary evil, the use of which is to be avoided whenever possible. When it must be employed, he should use it sparingly and in minimum amounts.

Driers are substances which have a powerful chemical or catalytic effect on the drying of linseed oil. They promote and accelerate the initial drying of the oil film; they counteract the slow-drying effect certain pigments have on linseed oil, also the slow drying or anti-drying effect produced by some varnish-oil mixtures.

Cobalt drier, made of cobalt naphthenate or cobalt linoleate and thinned to usable fluid consistency with turpentine or mineral spirit, is the only artists' drier approved by modern authorities. Its use must be limited to normal or very thin paint films; it should not be used in thick, impasto painting; when it is necessary, it should be added in minimum amounts —just the fewest number of drops which will produce the effect. Excessive amounts of drier will detract from the permanence of the paint and lead to cracking, darkening, and other defects. Instead of adding a set amount of drier to a recipe it is well to make trials and reduce the amount to the minimum quantity which will dry the mixture satisfactorily.

The pigments themselves exert a drying or retarding effect on linseed oil, although this varies to a considerable degree— for example, the umbers and white lead will dry rapidly, whereas cadmium yellow and zinc white dry slowly. Most manufacturers of oil colors add minute amounts of cobalt drier to the very slow-drying colors in order to bring them a little closer to the average drying time of the rest of the palette.

NOTES ON OIL-PAINTING METHODS

Preliminary drawings or outline sketches on the canvas are generally done with light pencil strokes or with charcoal, the excess grains of which are tapped away or flicked off with a cloth. It is often desirable to have these guide lines rather strong and resistant to the paint; in this case they are gone over with a pointed brush and a very much thinned-down oil color which dries rapidly (for example, burnt umber plus about an equal amount of thinner), and allowed to dry.

When methods used are more complicated than the simple direct oil painting technique, such as a first underpainting which is allowed to set, or the use of thin glazes, or any multiple-layer technique—there is sometimes doubt as to the advisability of unrestricted free painting into or over surfaces which are wet, semi-dry, or completely dry. Investigators have suspected that some of these manipulations might lead to eventual cracking of the paint, because of interference with the normal drying action of the oil and the slowness of its conversion from the fluid stage to the tough hard film of dried paint. However, with well-made oil colors, correctly ground with cold-pressed linseed oil, it seems safe to paint freely in any of these ways, provided that the simple rules as outlined on page 131 are observed. There has been no objection on the part of chemists on the score of painting into or over wet, or semi-dry or sticky paint; but the statement has been made—on the basis of some laboratory tests—that it is inadvisable to paint over recently or freshly dry coatings, and that once a paint film has become surface-dry it is better to wait until the layer is thoroughly dry before overpainting, usually several weeks.

This thorough drying is undoubtedly necessary with poppy oil colors, which should be used only for simple, direct, *alla prima* painting. However, the best grades of linseed oil colors, which are less critical in this respect, will withstand this departure from theoretically correct treatment; and unless very heavy, enormously exaggerated impasto is freely used, artists find that they can paint over recently dried underpainting without bad results.

Use of medium. No painting medium is required for simple, direct oil painting, and it is a mistake to use complicated mixtures or techniques either to make up for a lack of skill in manipulations or to make special effects easier to obtain. It is for this reason that the mediums mentioned in this chapter have been called glaze mediums rather than painting mediums;

they are more useful and more necessary for thin, transparent glazing or extremely thin overpainting than for use in more solid, average, or heavy painting, which is generally better thinned with plain turpentine or mineral spirit.

The majority of experienced painters prefer to mix their own glaze mediums because so many of the ready-made mediums of the shops are put out as secret formulas without a clear statement of all their ingredients. Variation or adjustment of home-made mixtures to suit individual requirements is easy; with ready-prepared mediums it is dangerous.

Ingredients of glaze mediums. Among the approved materials for use in painting or glaze materials are two specially refined linseed oils—stand oil and sun-refined oil.

Stand oil is a pale, very viscous product of honey-like consistency, made by a high temperature process and also known as polymerized oil. Stand oil is non-yellowing, and when thinned down to usable consistency works well in mediums. It has a tendency to flow out smoothly to an enamel effect.

Sun-refined oil is made by exposing linseed oil to sunlight until it is clarified, bleached and somewhat thickened. If desired, it can be thickened to a heavy viscosity. Sun-refined oil has always been used by artists for use in mediums, and sometimes oil colors have been made with it (see page 40), but the specially treated oils of this type are ordinarily not well adapted to color grinding. Sun-refined oil is a fairly quick drier whereas stand oil dries very slowly and usually requires an addition of a little cobalt drier when used in mediums. Stand oil is more reliable than sun-refined oil in non-yellowing properties; some samples of sun-refined oil have been observed to revert to a deeper color when stored in bottles.

The following resinous ingredients are in approved use for glaze mediums.

Damar varnish, a solution of damar resin in turpentine, described further on in this chapter.

Venice turpentine, an extremely thick, viscous fluid resin or oleoresin. It is the exhudation of a certain species of European larch, which over the centuries has been found to be one of the few oleoresins of its kind that give good results and complies with all the requirements for use in permanent oil painting mediums.

Some typical recipes for glaze mediums are as follows (the first one gives good results for all-round purposes and is in wide use):

(1)   Stand oil   1 fluid ounce
        Damar varnish   1 fluid ounce
        Turpentine   5 fluid ounces
        Cobalt drier   15 drops

(2)   Damar varnish   4 fluid ounces
        Sun-refined linseed oil   2 fluid ounces
        Venice turpentine   1 fluid ounce
        Turpentine   4 fluid ounces

The manipulative properties of such mediums can be altered to meet individual requirements by slight changes in the proportion of oily and resinous ingredients. Increasing the varnish content will give a more sticky or tacky quality, and decreasing it will make it handle in a more oily way.

Glazing and scumbling. Glazing is a method of imparting color effects to a painting by superimposing a thin layer of transparent or nearly transparent color over a dried, colored or monochrome painting. The glaze heightens and increases the color and brightness of the underpainting rather than obscuring it. The blended effect of this kind of coloring is entirely different from that in which two colors are mixed or scrambled into each other, and one can hardly be imitated by the other. Note the enormous variation in color effect between the transparent and opaque methods of handling burnt sienna in the frontispiece. The effect of the transparent E cannot be matched by mixing the color with white, as in F.

Formerly there was much difference of opinion as to the relative advantages of glazing versus solid painting as a regular technique, but today glazing is generally recognized as a legitimate tool or technique to be employed whenever the artist wishes to obtain its special effect. It may be used either to produce smooth, blended effects or to enliven the color of more casual or roughly stroked areas of paint.

Fundamentally, glazes should follow the rule for brightness as applied to grounds on page 19, that is, applying them over brilliant, reflective undercoats. However, there are so many variations and effects in which glazing may be used to advantage that no generalized instructions can be given in this respect.

Oil colors may be squeezed out of their tubes onto ordinary writing paper and allowed to remain there for a short while. This will absorb some of the surplus oil. Then they can be removed with the palette knife and mixed thoroughly with the glaze medium on a dish or palette to the desired consistency; for average use it should be quite fluid.

These glazes are then applied to a dried oil or tempera painting in a very thin, transparent manner with rather dry brush strokes, or by uniform careful stippling with the brush held vertically or with a cloth dabber. For accurate, precise work the painting is sometimes removed from the easel and laid flat on a table.

Scumbling means coating a dried painting by rubbing over it with a little straight oil paint, usually but not necessarily smearing or rubbing off the surplus with a soft cloth or the fingers. Scumbling implies the use of light or pale tints over darker ones, the use of opaque instead of transparent pigments and sometimes a rather wholesale, over-all toning rather than the carefully controlled, more delicately applied glazes.

Special effects. The best way to insure permanence in oil painting is to keep the process simple, not to stray too far from the simple rules and regulations when painting with linseed oil colors and to obey them very carefully when using poppy oil colors. The attempt to duplicate some of the effects of the seventeenth century Flemish artists has led some painters into complex and troublesome procedures, when, as modern investigators have so often pointed out, the materials of these older painters in the oily mediums were not so very different from ours. Their oil paints were perhaps somewhat more fluid and less stiff or plastic than ours; resinous painting or glazing mediums were added to them only when thin glazes and other special manipulations were involved. Sometimes, however, an effect created in certain areas, especially where white lead and flesh tones and other pale tints made with white lead were used, display crisp linear or impasto definition which defies reproduction when we use the more softly blending whites which we now buy in tubes.

One simple way of altering the properties of our flake or Cremnitz white tube color is to mix in a little egg yolk by working it into the paint thoroughly with the palette knife. If not used to excess, this seems to be a safe way of obtaining the desired crispness. The egg must be added a little at a time until the desired painting qualities are obtained; an excess will throw the mixture over to an oil-in-water emulsion or tempera paint. For the same reason, neither turpentine nor water should be added during the mixing, although the paint may be freely diluted with turpentine during its use. This mixture is a dual emulsion in which oil is the surrounding medium or external phase, and it can be handled and thinned like any other opaque oil paint except that it dries or sets up more rapidly.

Another means of achieving this crisp handling quality is to grind to paste consistency titanium or zinc white in whole egg and mix two parts of it with two to three parts of flake or Cremnitz white oil color. Some artists use an egg-and-oil tempera emulsion such as the one mentioned on page 000 instead of straight egg; the entire procedure requires a little experimentation to suit the individual's personal requirements, and the resulting dried paint films have to be carefully examined to see whether or not they are tough and flexible enough before adopting any such mixture of materials for continual use, especially on canvas. Casein paints will also mix with oil colors in the same way, but the combination of casein and linseed oil is not recommended because of rapid after-yellowing and embrittlement of such mixtures on aging.

Throughout the nineteenth century a number of complex painting mediums were added to oil paints in order to alter their brushing qualities, and virtually all these have been discarded because of the rapid decay of the paintings in which they were used. Chief among these offenders was a jelly-like substance with a curious name, *megilp*. Made by mixing heavy mastic varnish with a linseed oil that had been cooked to blackness with litharge, this material was used with oil paints to impart a brushing quality that overcame many difficulties, at the almost certain cost of the eventual disintegration of the painting. Until modern technology supplies us with new materials, it would seem that the wisest course to follow is to avoid all departures from the simple oil-paint technique and to use painting mediums sparingly.

Overpainting. The technical term, *pentimento,* refers to a peculiar effect, examples of which are to be seen in galleries, where because thin top coatings of paint have become more transparent with age, the underpainting or drawing originally concealed has become visible. Notable or striking examples of pentimento are seen in some of the works of De Hooch, where the bold black-and-white checkerboard of floor tiles occasionally shows through the figures and furnishings in the room. They are found also in early Italian paintings where the architectural lines of buildings may sometimes be discerned running through the figures that have been superimposed over them.

Such effects also are commonly seen in more recent pictures where the artist has made changes during the painting and, in obliterating unwanted brushwork or altering contours by overpainting, has been so careless in making these changes that, on relatively short aging, the colors underneath have become visible or the texture of underlying brush strokes has become more pronounced.

Although it may take such notable examples to bring home the fact that paint is likely to become literally transparent with the years—because of the increase of the refractive index of linseed oil film with age or for other reasons—the general effect of transparency exists in all old paintings. The lessons which careful painters have learned from this are several: that multiple layers of paint must be planned with this effect in mind; that when underpainting is to be concealed or obliterated, the top coat must be sufficiently opaque for the purpose; that when the underpainting is intended to be a definite part of the final effect, color and forms should be planned so that any change caused by the overpainting's becoming still more transparent will enhance rather than detract from the effectiveness of the whole. The underpainting and the ground always exert some influence on the final effect.

Overpainting of old canvases. As mentioned on p. 64, artists are often tempted to paint new pictures on top of old ones; and some are continually searching for a means to prepare an old surface for that purpose, either for the sake of economy or because of remoteness or shortage of supplies. The answer to this problem is "don't." Although drastic changes can be made during the painting of a picture by careful planning or the scraping down of paint (while still fresh enough to remove heavy brushstrokes easily), a completely dried painting—which bears forms, colors, and especially irregularities of thickness that have no relation to the overpainting—cannot be used as a foundation for permanent and successful results; the original design will soon strike through the newer work. However, if the film is fresh enough to be removable with a palette knife, scraping down the old paint will give good textural or structural finish on which to paint, provided that color effect is satisfactory.

Prepared paint removers will deposit paraffin wax on the surface and their powerful solvents will weaken the supporting oil film or ground. When, despite its disadvantages, an old canvas is used for a new painting, perhaps the use of a high-grade flat paint as mentioned on page 91 is as good a coating as any to obliterate the old work, since the complex coating structure of the finished work will, at best, not be permanent or stable.

Oil painting on paper. Oil paintings, especially those of small size, are sometimes attempted on paper or paper which has received some sort of coating to render its surface less absorbent or more adaptable to the medium. Paper is a completely unsuitable material for oil paint from almost any viewpoint—it lacks structural strength and stability, it is alien and inappropriate to the oil medium, and the resulting works are usually very fragile. Almost every oil painting on paper that subsequently is found to be of artistic merit and worthy of preservation has to receive extensive and sometimes drastic restoring treatments because of the embrittlement of the paper or some other defect.

VARNISHES AND VARNISHING

A varnish is a clear solution of a resin in a volatile solvent; a typical example is damar varnish which is a solution of damar resin in turpentine. Three kinds of varnish are used by artists: picture varnish, retouch varnish, and mixing varnishes used as ingredients of painting mediums.

Resins are insoluble in water, but will dissolve and mix with various organic solvents and oils. There are many commercially useful resins which are hardened exudations from many sorts of forest and crop-grown trees, as well as a number of treated or modified natural resins and several different types of synthetic or man-made resins.

Resins vary greatly in properties such as appearance, hardness, durability, and solubility in various solvents. Only a small number of them have been used in artists' materials and only a few of these have survived the test of time, remaining in current, approved use. Chief among those satisfactory for use in picture varnishes are damar, mastic, and the methacrylate (acrylic) resins, from which simple turpentine solutions may be made. Damar, Venice turpentine, Strassburg turpentine and the non-yellowing alkyds may be used in glaze mediums.

The outmoded resins, which have long since been discarded because they do not conform closely enough to the requirements of an ideal material for artists' varnishes, include materials one may read of in older books, such as: rosin, burgundy

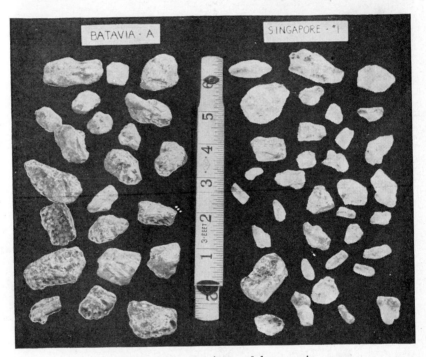

FIG. 39. Average specimens of damar resin.

pitch, sandarac, elemi, kauri, amber, and the various copals, hard and soft. Many of these resins, as well as a number of more modern synthetic resins have been rejected because they will not dissolve in turpentine, or they cannot be made into varnish unless cooked with oils, plasticizers, and driers, or because they will eventually turn yellow or crack. Most of them, however, have other good properties which make them valuable for certain uses in industrial varnishes and enamels. In industry, the copals and other natural resins have largely been superseded by modern synthetic resins with superior properties.

Picture varnish. A picture varnish is a necessary final coating for the preservation and uniform appearance of an oil painting. In order to make certain that the normal drying process of oil paint is not hampered, it has been the custom to wait six months or a year, depending on how heavily the paint was applied, before varnishing; but with a painting of thin or average thickness of layers, it would be less harmful to varnish a little too soon than to chance the picture's remaining unvarnished for too long a period.

This question of premature varnishing is not nearly so serious or important as artists have been given to believe; a picture does not run very much risk of damage if it is varnished soon after it has become thoroughly dry to the touch or surface-dry. It was a more serious consideration in the recent past, when copal or very thick glassy coatings of mastic varnish were applied; these were quite capable of injuring a tender or soft paint layer by the great strain which was put upon the surface by the contraction or compression of their drying. Nowadays a thinly brushed-out varnish is the rule; those smooth, glassy finishes are considered less desirable than the normal oil-paint gloss which a more thinly applied varnish gives.

An unvarnished painting, even if it is uniform in sheen when first dried, will frequently become spotty within a few months; its color effect will suffer not only from the dull, sunken-in spots but also from the distorted color relationship between the various areas, some of which will retain their gloss longer than others.

Dirt will settle into the surface of an unvarnished painting and, with the passage of time, will become so embedded that cleaning becomes difficult and sometimes impossible. A varnished painting is easily kept clean by occasional dusting and, should the varnish become seriously encrusted with dirt after an accumulation of years, it may be cleaned and the dirt removed. Methods for the cleaning of paintings are described on page 128. Varnish prolongs the life of paintings by preserving them not only against dirt but also against the ravages of time, moisture, mold and wear.

A picture varnish should be freely soluble in turpentine or mineral spirit. Varnishes which require stronger solvents are likely to attack the oil film while being applied; also they will usually evaporate too rapidly to allow of satisfactory brush manipulations. If it ever becomes necessary to remove a varnish that requires a strong solvent or some other drastic means the painting will be endangered. Turpentine, or mild petroleum solvent will not harm well-dried paint. Good picture varnish must be composed of nonyellowing resins, not too hard or brittle in nature, and it must present a uniform gloss when properly applied.

Kinds of picture varnish. The two best picture varnishes are a simple solution of damar resin in turpentine, and a simple solution of methacrylate resin in volatile petroleum solvent or turpentine. The next best is a simple solution of mastic resin in turpentine. Mastic is rated somewhat below the other two because of its tendency to turn somewhat yellow with age, its greater tendency to crack and to bloom (the formation of a white or bluish white fogginess), and also because of the more glassy effect of its finish.

Damar varnish is a pale straw-colored liquid, seldom absolutely clear in the bottle. This is due to natural waxes which give it a slightly cloudy appearance before application, but which will dry perfectly clear. Mastic is perfectly clear in the bottle, but it has a more amber tinge. The pure methacrylate or acrylic varnishes are water-white, clear, fast-drying, and yield a more uniform surface with a duller gloss than do the others.

Home-made varnish. No cooked oil varnishes or heat-treated oils should ever be attempted by amateur varnish makers, but some of the cold-cut or simple solution types can be made easily. The synthetic resins are not generally available at present, and their compounding must be left to expert technicians.

Damar and mastic varnishes may, however, be advantageously made by suspending a cheesecloth bag of the crushed resin in a container of pure gum spirit turpentine (Figure 41) for 24 to 36 hours (Figure 42), removing it (Figure 43), and, if necessary straining it through cotton sheeting, and keeping it in tightly capped bottles. If accuracy of recipe is important, the container can be a more tightly closed kind, to minimize evap-

FIG. 40. Group of materials used in making damar or mastic varnish.

oration of the solvent (Figure 44). The usual proportion for damar is 6¼ ounces of resin to 10 fluid ounces of pure gum turpentine. This is known as a "5 pound cut," being the equivalent of 5 pounds to 1 gallon. For mastic, 8 ounces to 10 fluid ounces of turpentine is customary. The correct consistency for a varnish is best measured by judging its feel when put to actual use, adding a little thinner if it is too thick or sticky, and making it stronger if it is too thin or watery, rather than too strict reliance on accurately measured recipes.

It must always be borne in mind that the color of oils or varnishes cannot be judged or compared to each other unless they are viewed in identical bottles, because the greater bulk or

FIG. 41. Making varnish: Placing the resin in its solvent.

volume of the liquid in a large bottle will make it seem darker than the same liquid in a smaller one. Figure 46 shows a test for comparing the *viscosity* of two oils or varnishes. By inverting the two cylindrical bottles and observing the speed with which the bubbles travel to the top, an accurate comparison can be obtained. Identical bottles, filled to the same level, must be used.

FIG. 42. Making varnish: The resin being dissolved.

Retouch varnish. Retouch varnishes are intended to be used during painting, or when retouching a dried painting. This is necessary in order to bring the dry areas or any sunken-in places up to the normal gloss of a wet, freshly painted surface, so that colors can be accurately matched or manipulated. The

gloss and color effects in dry oil paint are almost always somewhat different from those of fresh, wet paint (see pages 22 and
23) and the two must be brought to the same degree of gloss in

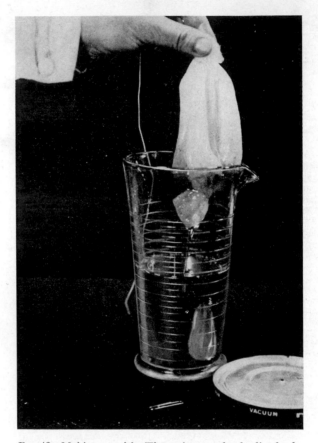

FIG. 43. Making varnish: The resin completely dissolved.

order to have the final color effects of the new paint the same
as that which has already dried.

Retouch varnish is made of nonyellowing resins, similar to
picture varnish, but it contains very much more turpentine or
petroleum solvent and is much thinner, because a retouch var-

nish should act more as a size (see page 75) than as a film-producing varnish coat. For example, a full-bodied picture varnish creates a definite continuous layer of resin on the picture; this would add complications to its structure, besides

FIG. 44. Making varnish: Dissolving the resin in an airtight container.

making a doubtful anchorage for the new paint, and introducing undesirable glossy areas. A high-grade retouch varnish should have no more effect on a picture than its function of supplying a temporary gloss; the amount of resin it deposits on the picture is inconsequential and will have no harmful effect

on either the structural permanence or appearance of the painting. If correctly and thinly applied, the gloss effect will be

FIG. 45. Varnish brushes.

temporary, merging with the general uniform appearance of
the canvas, or disappearing entirely after a short time.

Retouch varnish is best stroked on lightly with a soft brush.
It can be made so that it will dry rapidly, remain glossy and

tacky for a few hours, or dry very slowly—thirty hours or more. Most, if not all, of the materials on the market, dry within 4 to 6 hours depending on the absorbency of the surface. Sticklers for details in performance demand expensive retouch var-

FIG. 46. Comparing the viscosity of two samples of oil or varnish.

nishes which have been delicately formulated to meet very exacting requirements, but very often the painter may use a much thinned-down solution of damar varnish and turpentine.

Varnishing paintings. A wide, flat bristle brush (varnish brushes are described on page 197) is usually employed to varnish paintings. The painting and brush must be completely free from moisture; painting, brush and varnish must all be at room temperature. All varnishing must be done with the picture lying flat, never in a sloping or vertical position. The varnish must be well worked into the surface and spread out thinly and uniformly. The brushing out and smoothing operations must be done with dispatch, so that the varnish does not set up or dry irregularly, but not so rapidly or violently as to whip up air bubbles.

Picture varnish is generally sold ready to use but before varnishing, the consistency or viscosity is tested, to make sure that it is not too sticky or thick for easy brushing; if it is, turpentine is stirred in cautiously and in small amounts until it is just right. A too-thin consistency is not desirable either, as a sufficient body is necessary to retain uniformity of gloss and to avoid dripping and other surface defects.

After varnishing, the work is allowed to dry in a level, horizontal position until the varnish sets up and becomes tacky (10-15 minutes), after which it can be leaned against the wall, face in, to dry out completely.

Attempting to apply final picture varnish with a mouth blower will introduce too much moisture into the film—a sure way to produce bloom—but it may be applied in smooth, flawless coats by the use of a power-driven spray gun with a moisture trap. In experienced hands this is an ideal method, but such machines are seldom available to artists.

Cleaning paintings. The cleaning of paintings is, in general, more a matter of skill and experience than a simple knowledge of the right and wrong materials to use, and all complex operations are better left to the professional or expert restorer.

Contrary to popular notions, water or a damp cloth is not always a safe material for cleaning oil paintings. It should not be used on old, dry, cracked paint surfaces because of the likelihood of moisture seeping through and loosening the glue sizing in the ground. When water must be used, little balls of absorbent cotton should be well-squeezed so that they are just damp. After cleaning, the painting must be thoroughly and completely dried before varnishing. Soap is often destructive and should not be used by non-professionals on paintings.

The safest cleaning fluids are turpentine, mineral spirit, naphtha, or benzine which will not harm completely dried, sufficiently aged oil paintings. No liquids should be allowed to flood a painting; they are applied by moistening wads of absorbent cotton as described in the preceding paragraph. Simple, soft-resin picture varnishes, such as methacrylate and damar varnishes, can be removed with turpentine or mineral spirit to the point where the painting will be sufficiently bright and clean; it is neither necessary nor desirable to remove every trace of old varnish. Removal of hard varnishes such as copal, as well as other difficult surface conditions, require alcohol or other stronger solvents. These should not be used by inexperienced persons. Spots, spatters of paint, unwanted brush strokes, and encrusted foreign matter, however, are usually easy to remove by scraping with a sharp blade such as a small scalpel or surgeon's knife.

Freshly painted or recently dried paintings often will not resist the action even of the mild solvents; such canvases can usually be cleaned with balls of white bread kneaded from the center of a fresh loaf and used like an art eraser; care must be taken to remove all traces of bread from the surface so that it does not encourage the growth of mold.

Defects of oil paintings. Properly executed oil paintings that have been properly cared for will survive hundreds of years without cracking, peeling, flaking, blistering, or exhibiting any of those defects or failures which sometimes occur in cases where the rules for correct execution and care have been ignored.

Cracking is caused by (1) painting brittle layers over flexible layers; (2) use of inferior materials; (3) long storage in bad atmospheric conditions (too cold or too hot, too damp or too dry); and (4) sharp or sudden bending or rolling of canvas or warping of panels.

Flaking, peeling and blistering (usually preceded by crack-

ing) is caused by (1) lack of sufficient adhesion between layers
or between paint and ground (see page 104); (2) moisture at-
tacking from front or rear of paint.

Yellowing of oil paintings. Good oil paintings do not become
yellowed with age; some linseed oils will actually bleach on
long exposure to daylight. A slight degree of yellowing which
may be observed in dried *clear* linseed oil films is masked by
the pigment when the same oil is made up into a paint. When
the oil is improperly used, however, or when the wrong grade
of oil is selected, a definite after-yellowing can occur.

The outmoded practice of "oiling out" a dried painting with
linseed or poppy oils by rubbing the clear oil over the painting with a cloth has been responsible for much yellowing of
old paintings; no clear coatings of oil or oil varnishes should
be used in permanent painting techniques. The yellowed or
brown appearance of old pictures is most frequently caused by
dirt and by discoloration from old varnish; after these are removed the oil paint is generally found to be in its original
bright condition.

Oil paint will sometimes turn yellow if the freshly painted
work is allowed to dry in total or nearly total darkness. A
painting should be exposed to normal daylight (but not in the
direct rays of hot sunlight) during the two or three weeks of
its initial drying time, after which it can be safely stored in a
darker place. If a painting has yellowed because of absence of
light while drying, it may be brought back to its original state
by a period of exposure to normal daylight. This reversible
photogenic behavior of linseed oil was known to artists at least
as far back as the seventeenth century. Some kinds of linseed
oil are more sensitive in this respect than others; the common
industrial white lead in oil is quite susceptible to the action,
and painting grounds made with it *always* should be allowed
to dry in daylight.

Highly bleached, straw-colored paint-grinding oils (acid-re-
fined) will revert back to an amber color on aging, whereas the
normal golden amber, cold-pressed oil will not change. Stand

oil and some of the modern "varnish-refined" oils of low acid number are also nonyellowing. A warm, humid atmosphere promotes the tendency of linseed oils to yellow when drying in the dark.

Care of oil paintings. Oil paintings should be preserved under the same normal indoor surroundings generally considered as comfortable, average living conditions; excessively cold, dry, or humid atmospheres and sudden changes in temperature and humidity should be avoided.

The best way to protect a canvas from the rear is to tack a piece of cardboard of the same size to the stretcher frame. This is better than coating the canvas, and it also protects the painting from mechanical damage; it insulates it from sudden atmospheric changes, and keeps out most of the dust and dirt. Very tight or hermetic sealing of the cardboard is not advisable.

The practice of rolling canvases and repeated removal and re-stretching puts a great strain on paintings, it is likely to lead to cracking, and should be avoided as much as possible. It is much better to store and transport un-stretched canvas flat, than to roll them.

SIMPLE RULES FOR PAINTING IN OIL

The following concise outline touches on the more important points to be observed.

1. Use a white ground which is firmly anchored to its support.

2. Canvas should be prepared with oil grounds; emulsion or gesso grounds belong on panels.

3. Be sure there is good adhesion between paint and ground.

4. Use sufficient paint to produce a full, normal paint coating so that the final picture has the desired paint quality, but do not overload the work with extremely thick or exaggerated impasto. Avoid, at all costs, a continuous, thick, pasty layer of paint; heavy or thick impasto strokes are best used in isolated spots.

5. Remember the basic rule for all paint coatings and layers,

that is, always paint flexible coats over less flexible layers, and never use brittle coatings over flexible ones.

6. The degree of absorbency and texture of the ground should be suited to the type and kind of painting. Control of the paint and permanence of results is greatly influenced by this.

7. Thin the paint with a little turpentine when desired; avoid the habitual use of painting mediums and emulsion-stiffened whites except when the occasion calls for glazes and special effects.

8. Remember that previous painting or underpainting has some effect on the final results and that careless overpainting may lead to unwanted effects.

9. Oil paintings must be varnished eventually. It is desirable to wait 3 to 6 months before varnishing, but it is better to varnish them too soon than to put them into circulation or exhibit them unvarnished.

HISTORICAL

The practice of easel painting in oil paint on canvas has been universal since the seventeenth century; it did not arise as a sudden invention, but was the result of a long development. Scholars have traced this development in considerable detail through the various schools of art, and the subject can be studied by reference to the books listed in the bibliography. There are several milestones or turning points in the history of European easel painting which can be noted briefly as follows:

The early tempera paintings, notably those of Italy, were done on gesso grounds on wood panels. Working under the patronage of the Church or the reigning families, the artists reflected the artistic tastes of their times. The results achieved were exactly what the painter desired; the rather limited effects and the rather intractable materials were manipulated by developing superior skill and craftsmanship rather than by adopting more fluent or easily handled materials. Giotto is an outstanding example of the early Italian painters in this tradition; the works of Botticelli and Fra Angelico exemplify the high point of technical achievement in pure egg tempera.

A subtle change then follows; as small amounts of waxy, oily or resinous materials began to be introduced into the tempera in various ways, paintings showed a definite degree of technical change. These were characterized by a somewhat more fluent command of brushwork and a trace of softening or blending of colors, but for the most part they retained the same dry, linear quality of the earlier type. The final culmination of this later type of tempera painting may be seen in the work of the Venetian painters of the fifteenth century—such as Antonello, Domenico Veneziano, and Andrea del Castagno—who refined their tempera paintings throughout with oily or resinous transparent glazes. Also, in the Northern countries, following the innovations of the Van Eycks and others at Bruges, the works of van der Weyden, van der Goes and Memling show the use of oil glazes over tempera underpaintings carried on to the highest degree of jewel-like perfection.

The artist has two instruments which he uses to express his intentions in paint; they are line and color or tonal masses. In their importance to painting techniques neither one can be rated above the other, and when discussing them the same general terms are applied to each. Two completely different technical approaches may thus be distinguished.

In the first, the line predominates and the painters cited in the preceding paragraph always retained completely and meticulously their original draftsmanship. Underpainting was never entirely obscured by the final painting; its effect had a strong and direct influence on the finished work. The pictures are by no means colored drawings; they are veritable paintings, but the color or tonal element is subordinate to the linear quality.

The next great change was the tendency to techniques in which the tonal masses could be made to contribute a greater influence toward the final effect so that they might be used to play a part equal to that of the linear draftsmanship, or if desired, to dominate the total effect. This change, which came about through the demands and requirements of changing times and conditions, rather than by the "discovery" of new materials or methods, was made possible by the adoption of oily mediums as opposed to the aqueous tempera which is more suited to the linear or "drier" kind of painting. The oily paints, which dry more slowly and which are adapted to a more plastic handling, are more versatile. Blending of tones, and also a looser, more fluent stroking, may be used if desired, and the final coats of paint can be made to contribute the major part of the total effect, whereas in the earlier method, the under-painting or drawing predominates.

Because of the gradual and irregular state of development of the oil painting process and the varying requirements and conditions of schools and individuals in different localities during the fifteenth and sixteenth centuries, one cannot assign exact dates or chronological precedence to these changes.

However the development of the oil painting technique can be conveniently studied by observing the development of the painters whom we classify as belonging to the Venetian school and those who followed or came under its influence.

Giovanni Bellini, who started his career by painting in the traditional tempera manner, became a user of the oily materials later in his life and produced a more blended, flowing type of work. Following the previously mentioned painters, the works of Tintoretto and Titian display all the above-mentioned characteristics brought out by the increasing use of oily materials; although the disciplined and systematic training of the tempera painters is not wholly discarded, the fluency of oil paints creates a different type of picture. It is carried on still further by the technique of El Greco and finally that of Velasquez whose effects can be duplicated by the simple direct method we know today as straight oil painting.

In citing the names of some of the great masters of the past, it is not intended to imply that these men were necessarily the sole innovators or that only they possessed rare technical secrets; they are simply mentioned as convenient landmarks to illustrate the technical advances of their times and because they are universally known. They represent the culmination of the technical advances of their times.

In the work of Rubens, who had a prodigious command of technical facility, we find the culmination of all of the developments of Flemish and Italian techniques. Here the linear elements and tonal masses are combined and played against each other to bring one or the other into prominence at will. His paints were not of a complicated nature, differing in no major respect from our own except that they were perhaps more fluid. He is one of the most successful individuals of all time both in setting down his exact intentions and in securing lasting, permanent results. That he was not possessed of mysterious, technical secrets is amply shown by his writings and by those of his associates; in addition, by the fact that large numbers of his students, assistants and contemporaries used the same methods and materials. However, as an example of the culmination of a technique, his work is most interesting in marking another important change or landmark in the development of easel painting, that is, the deliberately planned and consistent use of comparatively thick or loaded opaque whites and pale colors combined with thinly painted or transparent darks and shadows. This makes for a distinct change or advance over the earlier type of work, in which for the most part, all color masses were painted in equal bulk or thickness. The use of this procedure can be discerned in the work of earlier painters but its adoption as a deliberate basic principle begins with this period.

In his choice of techniques, the present-day painter is guided by the experiences of the past, as to appropriateness of effects, permanence of results and the various materials which have proved themselves by the test of time, but he is no longer limited or confined to any single method or technique as were the painters of the past. All the accepted methods are available, and each is appreciated as a means of creating acceptable works of art; the styles of every age and every country now have their influences on our art, and their materials and techniques as well can be applied to our own purposes.

The use of entirely new materials or any innovations that can be applied to our modern developments in art proceeds rather slowly; we are still dependent on the traditional or time-tested methods of the past, and only a few of the modern innovations have been admitted to the lists of materials in widespread use. New processes which employ radically new materials and procedures have remained in the experimental stage and, at the present writing, our artists' materials, although supplemented by vastly improved grades of raw materials and a few new resins and pigments, have not progressed to any very considerable extent since Rembrandt's time.

This condition will probably remain until such time as an organized research program is carried out in the modern manner, so that the resources and facilities of modern paint technology can be drawn upon to supply us with the next important advance in our materials and tools. Any radical change in the working properties and permanence of our painting methods is more likely to come through the development of new materials than through a change in the handling of the traditional oils and resins.

Chapter 6

TEMPERA PAINTING

Description. Tempera paintings are done with paints which can be diluted freely with water, but which when dry become insoluble in water to the extent that they may be gone over with more tempera paints without being picked up. They yield pleasing textural and visual (optical) effects and are capable of much delicacy of control.

Tempera painting is capable of being applied to nearly any type of pictorial, decorative or abstract work but it is particularly suited to high-keyed or blond effects rather than to the deep-toned, intense or somber tones for which the straight oil painting method is more appropriate. Tempera paint can be applied in a completely opaque manner, and one may also get transparent results with it, but the special effect which distinguishes it from the other methods is a translucent, semi-opaque paint quality. Its handling is productive of a crisp, linear character which, combined with the luminosity and clarity of the color effect, gives results that cannot very well be duplicated by the use of any of our other standard methods.

Appropriate use of tempera. In general, tempera is more adaptable to a systematic, deliberately planned method of painting than it is to the casual or impulsive style. The advance preparation that goes into a successful work in tempera, both as to the painting procedure and the materials themselves, while not particularly onerous, appeal more often to the methodical painter than to one who prefers the more direct or immediate production of effects. If the control of a translucent quality in the paint and brushwork is maintained, the brilliant ground, the original modeling, and the various colors of the underpainting all combine to contribute their effects to the final results.

Unlike water color and the usual direct oil techniques where color effect, draftsmanship and other elements of the work are simultaneous concerns of the painter, true tempera is a "division-of labor" method. The original drawing on paper should be complete and well-finished in detail, so that it may be used as a reference during painting. Either direct from life or assembled from notes and sketches, it should like a mural cartoon, have all problems of design, composition, draftsmanship and modeling worked out to their final degree so that painting, or the application of color will be unhampered by these considerations later on. This drawing is then transferred to or traced on a smooth gesso panel, made according to the methods outlined in Chapter 4, *Grounds*. Although the later stages of painting and overpainting can then be carried on calmly and without being complicated by decisions and alterations, it is not mechanical work, complete alertness is necessary to subdue and intensify color effect etc., one is freed only from decisions on the other elements. When it comes to the final layers or washes of color, much bold, spontaneous stroking can be used, thus overcoming any pickiness or labored effects that may have been introduced by the rigid control of the start.

Emulsions. Tempera paints owe their special characteristics to the fact that their vehicles are emulsions. A normal or customary emulsion is a homogeneous, stable mixture of an oily ingredient and an aqueous (dissolved in water) ingredient. In our general practical concept of materials, we say that oil and water won't mix, and this is perfectly true in the handling and mixing of the general run of fluids. However, under the proper circumstances, many oily (and this term includes fats, waxes and resins as well as oils) materials can be combined with water solutions if one or more of the ingredients is a good *emulsifier* or *stabilizer*. These emulsifiers are, for the most part, colloidal solutions of gums or gum-like materials.*

How emulsions are made. Some emulsions occur in nature and others may be made. The conditions for making an emulsion are: (1) the presence of an emulsifier or stabilizer of the correct type and (2) a thorough and vigorous agitation of the watery and oily ingredients. If, for example, a fairly viscous solution of a water-soluble gum is mixed with linseed oil and shaken or stirred together vigorously, the result will be a milky fluid in which the oil is uniformly suspended in myriads of minute droplets. The emulsion of oil and gum solution appears milky because of the diffuse reflection of light between the surfaces of all the little oil particles. For a similar reason snow appears white, as explained in the section on light (page 24). Upon drying, a film of this material will be as clear, or nearly as clear, as the original gum solution.

The little droplets in a good emulsion do not easily separate out and unite with each other, but remain dispersed during long storage. However, some of the approved emulsions, made in the necessary proportions for good tempera paints, may—on long standing in a bottle—show some degree of creaming. This is merely a heavy layer of emulsion, on top of a thinner layer which contains surplus water, and this separation should mix in promptly when the bottle is shaken, exactly as does the cream on a bottle of fresh milk.

Milk is an example of a natural emulsion, in which the oily ingredient (butterfat) is suspended in a solution containing casein and other materials which are good emulsifiers.

Emulsion types. There is another type of emulsion with which artists' paints are rarely involved, and that is a sort of reverse type in which the aqueous solution gets dispersed in the

---

* Gums are water-soluble substances mostly obtained as natural exudations from trees and shrubs, others are processed from various natural sources. The water-soluble gums should be distinguished from **Resins** (page 117) which are insoluble in water and which are used in varnishes. Some confusion exists because of the practice in the varnish trade of applying the term gum to varnish resins.

form of droplets and the oily ingredient acts as the surrounding medium. Butter is an example of such an emulsion, being composed principally of butterfat and water with small amounts of other ingredients. The usual or water-soluble emulsion is called an *oil-in-water emulson,* and the oil-soluble type is called *water-in-oil* emulsion. Although not frequently encountered, it is well to know that these oil-soluble emulsions exist, because under certain conditions they are likely to be formed, or one type is likely to invert over to the other type.

About the word "tempera." Some artists and commentators apply the word *tempera* to any opaque water paint such as the cheap poster colors, gouache colors, simple casein paints, etc., but this is incorrect. Such simple materials are not true tempera paints and will not behave in the same manner. The original meaning of the Italian word *tempera*—in the days when it was the principal method in use on artistic easel painting—came from the verb "to temper" and meant any liquid which could be mixed with pigments for binding and adhesive purposes, as distinguished from fresco painting in which the vehicle (pure water) has no binding or adhesive functions. In other words, the pigments were "tempered." At that time, oil paints were used only for coarser work, not for artists' easel paintings. After oil painting became the principal method in use by artists, the word began to be applied exclusively to emulsion paints. Some remarks concerning the historical development of tempera and its use in past ages will be found on page 132. The term *distemper,* which is not in general use in America, is applied to coarser water paints of the glue-size type; it denotes paints and painting for walls and other large-scale decorative purposes rather than artists' paints.

True tempera emulsion paints are not common in the shops and the carefully made ones are put up in tubes, never in jars. The use of the word *tempera* by manufacturers of poster colors in jars is misleading. Almost every type of tempera emulsion has been used to produce commercial tempera paints, particularly in the European brands. They have been made of emulsions based on egg, gum, casein-wax mixtures and combinations of various other ingredients; sometimes the materials or types are stated on the labels, but more often they are not. Each kind of tempera paint has its own special properties and some are more suitable for some purposes than others.

EGG TEMPERA

The original European tempera paintings were made on gesso panels with pigments ground in pure egg yolk diluted with water. Egg yolk is a perfect tempera-paint vehicle; it is a natural emulsion of an oily or fatty ingredient (called egg oil), with a water solution of a gummy ingredient called egg albumen, plus several lesser ingredients chief of which is lecethin, a powerful emulsion stabilizer. The method of painting tempera pictures completely by means of colors mixed with egg yolk and water is of considerable antiquity; by Giotto's time in the fourteenth century it had become well established, and we have many surviving examples as well as contemporary writings on the subject. It is one of the best documented of all the arts and crafts of the Italian Renaissance techniques which have come down to us. The most complete and interesting early manuscript on the subject is that of Ceninno Ceninni, who painted in the fourteenth century and whose treatise is available in modern translations. It is familiar to all artists who have made any study of painting materials and, besides the technical information it contains, it also affords many interesting glimpses into the character of the painter and the spirit of his times.

In connection with books of past ages, even up to works of the comparatively recent past, it is most important to remember to be very cautious in adopting these accounts as completely reliable, detailed guides for modern practice. Unless one is thoroughly grounded in the subject and can modify or discriminate between the finer points of good and bad, attempts at exhuming old recipes and "secrets" generally lead to disappointments.

FIG. 47. Separating the yolk from an egg.

FIG. 48. Removing egg-white from the yolk.

The pure egg-yolk technique, although limited in its manipulative properties and visual effects, appeals to many present-day painters who find that its special characteristics are adaptable to many modern requirements. The finished paintings have a luminosity and paint quality which cannot easily be matched precisely by other means.

FIG. 49. A method of handling the egg-yolk.

The following account of the traditional or classic pure egg-yolk technique is a basic instruction in tempera painting; all other tempera methods were developed from this method. Although modern painters frequently use other forms of tempera emulsions, its mastery is usually considered a necessary background for the practice and study of all tempera painting.

PREPARATION OF EGG TEMPERA PAINTS

Separating the yolk. Yolk of egg is considered an ideal tempera emulsion. Its ingredients are combined in proportions which, when well diluted with pure water, are well-balanced

FIG. 51. The yolk punctured and run into a jar.

FIG. 50. The yolk ready to puncture.

for the purpose. The painter, therefore, wants the pure yolk, uncontaminated by any of the white which is all albumen and would throw the properties off balance.*

The illustrations (pages 142 to 144) show a traditional way of extracting the pure yolk; after it is separated from the white (Figure 47), it is rolled dry on a towel (Figure 48), picked up (Figure 49) and held between the fingers of the left hand (Figure 50), then punctured by stabbing with a sharp point (Figure 51). Another method is simply to drop the yolks, after drying them, into a wire-mesh strainer to remove their skins. The yolk is easier to handle if the egg has been chilled.

The colors. Painting with egg-yolk on gesso requires a careful grinding of pigments and the use of at least as much water as egg in the final paint. Fresh egg-yolk must be used in tempera painting; therefore, to avoid the tedious task of grinding fresh paints every day, tempera colors are ground in water instead of in the yolk. The pigments are well ground to a paste or a syrupy consistency, either on a slab with a muller or in a mortar and pestle, until smooth and nongritty; they are then stored in small screw-cap jars, where they will keep indefinitely. A drop or two of weak phenol solution (from the drug store) may be added in order to prevent the growth of mold. If the colors were directly ground in egg-yolk, they would deteriorate rapidly because egg tempera paints will not keep for more than a day or two depending on climatic conditions. If for any special reason, the painter wishes to grind his pigments directly in a mixture of egg-yolk and water, there is no technical objection to it, except that the paint will harden or go bad in a day or two. The grinding is done in the same manner as the grinding of oil colors.

The approved list of pigments for tempera painting is the same as that employed in oil painting, listed on page 35 except that the leadbearing pigments (flake and Cremnitz white and

---

* With the exception of a few minor and highly specialized uses in the distant past, straight egg white has no place in the list of paint vehicles. In the egg-and-oil emulsions however, whole egg is commonly employed.

Naples yellow) may be used only when the finished painting is protected by oil or resinous paints, glazes, or varnishes.

Setting the palette. One measure of pure egg-yolk is mixed thoroughly with a palette knife on the palette or glass slab with about an equal volume of the water-ground pigment (Figure 52). This mixture is placed in a small jar and covered with a bit of cloth soaked in water which keeps it from drying out.

FIG. 52. Measuring color and egg-yolk.

Small amounts are transferred to the palette as required. A palette or plate, with small depressions to hold the rather fluid colors, or separate little cups are used; a hand-palette is not convenient. Some pigments occasionally (notably the blues) require a little additional egg or gelatin, in order to bind them securely. This can be ascertained by rubbing the paint with a soft cloth, after it has dried.

Painting in tempera. The painting is usually done directly on an absorbent gesso panel with red sable brushes. The colors are very freely diluted by continually dipping the brush in water. When completely dry, the surface can be polished to a dull, lacquer-like sheen by rubbing it with a wad of dry absorbent cotton. It may be varnished, waxed or overpainted with thin oil colors or glazes.

The traditional handling of tempera paints is usually a pencil-like brush stroking with the point of the brush—although if desired, broader masses may be applied as is often done in modern work. By diluting paint with much water during use its characteristic translucent quality is maintained, and solid, poster-like effects are avoided. The brush is ordinarily squeezed out between the fingers or a piece of Kleenex tissue so that the color does not flood the surface, and so that it does not form drops or dissolve the underpainting and the gesso. It is never scrubbed into the surface.

Its handling is neither like that of the thick, pasty oil paints which must be pushed about nor that of the free flooding water colors and gouache colors, but a special sort of flowing from a dryish brush—somewhat like pencil or pen manipulations.

Cennini's method was to strengthen and develop the original drawing by going over it with a fine brush, using three separately mixed shades of a mixed color like raw umber which he called *verdaccio,* and with which all the darks of the modeling were applied except on the portions of the panel underlying the flesh tones. These were given two veils or thin, transparent coats *(imprimatura)* of green earth and white; and then the modeling was put in with the darkest *verdaccio* used very thinly. The rosy or ruddy portions of the flesh were then underpainted with thin, transparent touches of pink made with vermilion to which a little white was added, and then the flesh color was applied in three ready-mixed shades, dark, medium and light, finally adding small touches or highlights of a very pale fourth flesh tint or white where required. The colors and mixtures were prepared in advance and kept in little cups.

While it is neither necessary nor desirable for the modern painter to be bound too closely by an ancient procedure such as this, reconstructions of the effects of the early painters will give the tempera painter an invaluable insight into all the potentialities of the medium toward adapting it to his own use.

The principal way to achieve the luminous and full tempera quality is to keep the colors fluid by using sufficient water, but at the same time to apply them with a dryish brush in the manner previously noted. Otherwise a dead, opaque quality will result and one may as well use gouache paints. On the other hand, the finishing strokes should not be too thin and unsubstantial like water-color washes or the veils used in the underpaintings. The bulk of the strokes should not be allowed to obscure the underpainting entirely, and all the layers of underpaintings should be permitted to contribute their effects to the final result.

Preservatives in egg. Experience has shown that the use of preservatives with home-made tempera colors is, in general, not successful. It is easier to add fresh yolk to the water-ground colors. The most frequently mentioned preservative is a few drops of a 5 per cent solution of acetic acid—or a few drops of vinegar (which usually contains about 5 per cent acetic acid). This solution will preserve egg yolk for a week or two, and has been used in the past, especially when tropical or excessively humid atmospheric conditions prevailed. The commercially prepared tempera colors usually contain preservative, but these colors are seldom if ever of the pure egg-yolk type, and the conditions involving the manufacture and distribution of commercial products vary greatly from those of home-made materials. Most experienced tempera painters dislike the use of preservatives.

OTHER TEMPERA EMULSIONS

Preparation. In order to make emulsions for tempera paints, other than the pure egg-yolk, one of the four pieces of equipment pictured in Figure 53 is used. The electric mixer is most efficient in the majority of cases; it will beat the oily ingredients into tiny droplets and produce speedy and thorough emulsification (Figure 54). An adequate but less efficient substitute is the kitchen egg beater. There is also another type of beater with an up-and-down plunger motion which is useful

when a recipe calls for gradual or drop-by-drop additions during the mixing since it requires only one hand to operate.
Shaking the ingredients in a half-to-three-quarters-full, tall-
shaped bottle is most useful for the mixing in of fluid ingredients as additions to emulsions, such as oil/egg emulsions.

FIG. 53. Four pieces of equipment used to make emulsions.

Grinding with a muller on a slab with small gradual additions
of one of the ingredients is best for stiff, "mayonnaise" type
mixtures and water-in-oil emulsions. In factories, the large-
scale mechanical equipment for making emulsions is based on
the same principles.

The following recipes are typical for tempera emulsions.

Egg and oil tempera

Whole eggs, stirred together with twice their volume of
water are strained to remove the skins and clots, then emulsi-

fied by shaking with ¼ its volume of an equal mixture of stand oil and damar varnish.

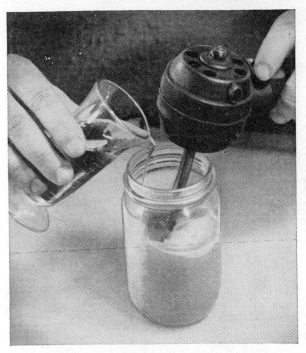

FIG. 54. Emulsifying with an electric mixer.

Gum tempera emulsion

    A—Aqueous ingredient:
        gum arabic ....4 ounces
        dissolved in hot water ....6 fluid ounces
    B—Oily ingredient:
        Damar varnish ....1½ fluid ounces
        Stand oil ....1 fluid ounce
    C—Plasticizer:
        Glycerin ....1 fluid ounce

A little more water in A produces a more fluid emulsion, sometimes preferred.

B is best added to A in a slow stream with constant strong stirring.

C is mixed into the finished emulsion.

Finishing tempera paintings. The glazing and varnishing of tempera paintings are carried out exactly as in oil paintings and may be done as soon as the water has dried completely out of the tempera film—in a day or so. The method calls for a thin coating of size (note precaution on page 75) to be brushed or sprayed over the painting in order to isolate it from the glaze which otherwise has too much tendency to sink in or become dull. A solution of white shellac very much thinned down with alcohol or a 5 per cent solution of gelatin in water are the usual sizing materials. The water solution is more difficult to use because of its tendency to pick up the underpainting. Most tempera paints can be polished to a smooth, lacquer-like gloss by rubbing with a soft cloth or a piece of absorbent cotton when dry and thoroughly set. If there is sufficient binder in the colors they will not rub off. Straight egg-tempera paintings, not glazed or overpainted with oils, may be cleaned with acetone but not with water.

Unlike faulty oil paints, which do not disclose their deficiencies and do not develop major defects until they have aged for a long time, faulty tempera paints will usually exhibit their shortcomings soon after drying. The permanence of standard, and even experimental, tempera paints can, as a general rule, be relied upon, provided that they dry promptly and show no evidences of failure on close examination after a day or two.

Mixed techniques. Tempera paints, particularly those made from emulsions of whole egg plus oil, are employed in combination with straight oil painting in several different ways. These complex techniques are used in order to obtain special effects which cannot easily be had by either oil painting or tempera painting alone. If a stroke of tempera paint is applied to freshly painted wet or tacky oil paint or oil plus varnish glaze, a crisply delineated effect is produced, entirely different in character from the results obtained by other means. If thin, transparent veils of tempera color are washed over a brilliant white gesso ground and the painting is built up with light and dark modeling, alternating and combining the effects of each of the oil and tempera mediums in both opaque and transparent ways, a great variety of textural and atmospheric effects may be produced. Provided that neither tempera nor oil strokes are applied with too much or too exaggerated thickness or impasto, and provided also that the paintings which contain more than just a little, occasional amount of tempera are done on panels instead of canvas, the mixed techniques can be considered permanent. They are not recommended for use by beginners or artists who are not familiar with both oil and tempera painting through first-hand experience.

Chapter 7

AQUEOUS PAINTS

WATER COLOR

The specific term *water color* refers to paintings done on a special hand-made rag paper with pigments very finely ground in a binding medium composed of a solution of gum arabic. Water-color paintings are done in a thin, transparent manner; pale tones are obtained by dilution of the paint with water, thus producing such a thin layer of pigment that the brilliant white effect of the paper is mingled with the color. This method of coloring generally is called the *transparent* or *glaze* system, and it is entirely different from the other coloring method called the *opaque* or *body-color* system (see page 112).

Modern moist water-color paints are sold in paste form in tubes and also in a stiffer, more solid form in pans. They are of equal value, tubes being more popular than pans because of convenience in handling. Originally, water colors were put up in hard, dry cake form, but for the past hundred years or so the popularity of these has steadily declined in favor of the moist colors and they have almost entirely disappeared from the shops.

Papers. All artists' paper should be made of pure linen or linen and cotton rags, free from wood pulp, chemical agents and resin fillers. The best water-color papers are hand-made by European firms of ancient descent; few American mass-production papers are useful for permanent work.

Water-color papers are sold in many grades and in a variety of textures and weights. The rough or "not pressed" finishes are the most popular and are the most desirable for average fine arts water colors; the smooth and hot-pressed finishes are more useful for other drawing and painting purposes.

The thinner kinds of water-color paper are best used when they are stretched by wetting them and adhering them to drawing boards with gummed paper strips along the edges or with paste. After they dry, painting can be done comfortably without the curling and buckling which takes place when loose sheets are used.

The thinnest grade of good water-color paper is known as "72-pound"; a medium lightweight grade, as "140-pound." The very heavy papers, designated as "300- to 400-pound," are preferred by many because they do not have to be stretched or mounted; they will not curl or buckle enough to bother the average painter and a superior paint quality or finish is produced upon them. The heavy papers will withstand much more drastic treatment than the lightweight grades, and many manipulations can be carried out on them that would ruin the thinner, more fragile sheets. Good papers are also made up into blocks or pads which are suitable for portable sketch use because of their compactness. These are not commonly obtainable in very large sizes.

Most water-color paper is sold in the "Imperial" size, the sheets measuring about 22 by 30 inches.

The mechanics of water color. Water-color paints are made by grinding pigments very fine in a gum arabic binding medium, together with certain necessary modifying ingredients. These ingredients usually are: (1) glycerin and honey (or sugar-syrup) which are plasticizers added in order to keep the colors moist and to improve their working properties; (2) a preservative to keep them from becoming moldy; and (3) a wetting agent such as ox-gall or Aerosol to make them take well and spread uniformly on the paper. The proportion of binder and pigment is very carefully balanced in order to give the paints exactly the correct properties. The tiny grains of pigment become embedded in the relatively coarse meshes of the paper and this action is of as much importance in holding the color to the paper as is the adhesive action of the gum binder (Figure 56). Water-color painting consists therefore of a very thin layer of pigment particles held just sufficiently to be a permanent coating; it is not a real paint film like a layer of oil paint, and therefore is not subject to some of the oil paint's defects such as cracking, peeling or blistering.

FIG. 55. Water-color paper. (Photomicrograph) the stripe is an ordinary pencil line.

FIG. 56. Normal water-color painting. (Photomicrograph.)

A careful balance of the modifying ingredients in water-color paints is necessary to give the correct working properties and to insure the proper balance of solubility; that is, the dried layer of a good water-color paint is sufficiently resistant so that it is possible to apply subsequent brush strokes without picking it up entirely. On the other hand the paint will not be so insoluble that it cannot be softened or run into when the painter so desires.

Transparent water colors are quite difficult to make successfully and the painter seldom attempts to make his own except under unusual circumstances. The best water colors of the shops leave little to be desired; their universal popularity has led to widespread availability and the development of a high degree of quality.

Gouache. A gouache painting is a water color done in opaque instead of transparent coloring; whites and pale tints are obtained by mixing titanium or Chinese (zinc) white with the colors instead of by utilizing the white of the ground. The *materials* used to make gouache and water-color paints are identical or nearly so, the difference between them lying in their method of preparation. Gouache pigments are ground with a greater proportion of vehicle to pigment, and when they are painted out the result is a continuous paint film of appreciable thickness rather than the thin wash or stain produced by water color (Figure 57).

Fig. 57. Normal gouache painting (Photomicrograph) showing film or layer character of the coating.

The color of the paper usually has little effect on gouache paint as an underlayer, and so sometimes a tinted paper is used for special effects, the exposed areas of the paper being utilized as a part of the color-scheme of the painting. Transparent water color is occasionally combined in a gouache painting; as a general rule this produces a better effect than when gouache is used in a picture which is predominantly water color. Some painters achieve a full range of textural and color effects by combining water color, gouache and pastel in the same picture. Gouache colors have a certain robust solidity which gives the effect of an impasto paint layer, heavier than that which actually exists and, therefore, the paint need not be piled up thickly. Because gouache paint is a real, continuous film with a non-too-flexible gum adhesive, it is likely to crack or peel off if applied too heavily.

A great variety of aqueous paints have been employed by artists to produce pictures popularly accepted as gouache paintings, for example, cheap poster colors, casein paints, tempera paints, water colors mixed with Chinese white, etc. True gouache paints, however, capable of being handled to give the best results in that technique, are made especially for the purpose, from the same gum solution and other materials used for water colors.

Unlike the transparent water colors, gouache paints may be easily and profitably made at home.

A typical water-color and gouache binder is made by adding to a 1:2 solution of powdered gum arabic, about ⅓ its volume each of glycerin and honey-water (1:1), a little ox-gall or Aerosol and a very small amount of preservative (page 166). Some gouache colors are improved—to a greater extent than are transparent water colors—if the vehicle in which they are ground contains a pasty adhesive in addition to the gum arabic binder. A stiff solution of white dextrin added to the gum solution will overcome the sticky or stringy consistency which is an occasional defect in some aqueous paints. The amount may be varied according to the requirements of each particular pigment, the result will generally be a smoother, more easily brushable paint. It is generally said however, that for finest and most sensitive professional use, the gum content should remain the principal ingredient in home-made gouache; the more dextrin used, the more the paint will tend toward the less delicate and less permanent poster-color type of paint.

Inert pigments, such as blanc fixe or chalk, are often ground in with some of the colored pigments, not as adulterants but in order to increase their bulk and to improve their brightness or opacity. Those colors which are ordinarily transparent in oil and water color act as body-colors in gouache, and often yield somewhat different color effects.

Casein paints. Casein, a powdered protein made from milk, has been mentioned as an adhesive and as a binder for grounds (page 88). Modern casein is an improved material made under scientifically controlled conditions, but it has long been used in a crude form, home-made from curd or pot cheese, and accounts of it are found in some of the earliest writings. It is an acceptable and permanent binding material. It has been quite successful in aqueous paints for a number of applications, but more so when they are compounded by expert technicians on an industrial scale than when home-made, for casein is a tricky material and one which is likely to yield erratic results unless used under carefully controlled conditions.

Casein powder is not soluble in water, but dissolves easily when ammonia is added. This is an advantage because, when a binder or adhesive made from casein has dried and the ammonia (a volatile material) has evaporated, the hardened material is much more resistant to water than glue or gum binders. When treated with certain chemicals (for example, spraying the finished coating with a 4 per cent formaldehyde solution), it becomes still more water-resistant, equaling egg tempera in this respect.

Paints made by grinding pigments in casein solutions are used for permanent painting in the gouache manner and also in mural painting in the fresco manner (see **Secco Painting**). Casein solutions are also used as tempera ingredients; they emulsify readily with waxes, resins and the vegetable oils, but the last-named are not to be recommended since all mixtures of casein and linseed oil become quite yellow on aging. Most authorities agree that casein is inferior to glue as a sizing material and binder for grounds because of its tendency to become brittle with age, and many painters rate it below the gum arabic type of water color or gouache paint in manipulative qualities and delicacy of control.

Typical recipe for dissolving casein. Allow an ounce of casein powder to soak in 6 fluid ounces of water overnight, then dissolve it by adding clear ammonia water, drop by drop with stirring, until the solution is as thick as honey and free from lumps or clots. For use as a paint binder add the preservative (⅛ to ¼ teaspoonful of sodium orthophenyl phenate (Dowicide A)) and thin to desired consistency with about 6 fluid ounces of water. For use in gesso, start with 4 ounces of casein, 24 fluid ounces of water, use ¾ teaspoon Dowicide A and dilute with about 3 quarts of water. This should bind 4 pounds of chalk or whiting to a satisfactory gesso. Casein gesso is used like glue gesso but in much thinner coats.

There is also a form of casein powder called mono-ammonium caseinate or soluble casein, which may be dissolved by warming it in water without adding ammonia. Sometimes this material loses its ammonia content on aging; then it requires the addition of ammonia, the same as with the regular casein.

Casein is widely employed in industrial products, among which there are a few of interest to the artist. Prepared casein wall paints sold in paste form are mentioned on page 91. Casein glue, sold as a prepared powder to be mixed with water, is a very powerful adhesive for joining wood. Recipes for the use of adhesives made from curd date back to the eleventh or twelfth century.

PERMANENT PALETTE FOR WATER-COLOR AND GOUACHE PAINTS

In the regular or pure water-color method of painting, almost all pigments are used for transparent or translucent effects, transparency being obtained from the more opaque paints by diluting them to a thin consistency. Paleness or whiteness of tone is obtained by utilizing the brilliant white of the paper showing through the colors instead of by the free, unlimited use of Chinese white mixed with the chromatic pigments to produce pale tints. The use of Chinese white in the pure water-color technique is either avoided entirely or confined to occasional touches for special effects. The vividness or deep tones of the strong colors in the painting are also enhanced by the underlying brilliant white ground, because they, too, are never applied in a thick or pasty manner.

In gouache painting all the pigments are compounded and used in a manner which makes them opaque, and in painting, the pale tints are obtained by mixing them with white paint. The color effects of all the pigments are those of their mass- or top-tones, and many of those pigments which exhibit their undertones when used in transparent oil or water-color paintings (such as burnt sienna or green earth) will therefore display a different color effect when used in the gouache technique.

The list of permanent pigments for water color and gouache is exactly the same as that used in oil painting (see page 35) with three exceptions. The lead-bearing pigments which are approved for use in oils—flake white, Cremnitz white and Naples yellow—are not used in water color because of their susceptibility to turning dark on exposure to impure air when not protected by oil or varnish; their likelihood of reacting with other pigments when used in the gum water mediums; and their poor brushing qualities in water mixtures.

GENERAL PROPERTIES OF AQUEOUS PAINTS

The paints made from pigments which have been ground with water vehicles require entirely different methods of brushwork and handling from those in which oil and varnish materials are used. As contrasted with oil paints, the technical handling of all aqueous paints (and their resulting pictures) have much in common. And yet the different varieties of water-soluble paints which are approved for permanent painting are distinctly different from one another, and each has its own characteristics that make it suitable for a particular kind of painting.

The bulk of the vehicle in an oil painting is linseed oil or, in some cases, a mixture of oils and resins; whatever volatile material may be used as a thinner (such as turpentine or petroleum solvent), is normally present in a relatively small proportion.

On the other hand, the binding ingredients of all the water mediums are very powerful adhesives and binders; even with the least powerful of these, the greatest bulk of a normal water paint, when it is ready for use, is water.

As has been noted, the oil vehicles do not evaporate, but remain in the dried paint film in approximately the same bulk as that which they occupied in the wet paint. Consequently, the pigment, still surrounded by a substantial excess of dried vehicle, will display the same or nearly the same color effect as did the wet paint. This same surplus vehicle also serves as a protective casing for the pigment. It has such flexibility, and such resistance to harm from moisture, temperature changes, cleaning agents, or wear and tear, that a well-made oil painting may be done on canvas, framed without glass and, if kept under the normal conditions of preservation which works of art are intended to receive, may be expected to survive for hundreds of years.

Paints made with water vehicles (as has been pointed out in commenting on the reasons for their mat effects as compared with the glossier oil paintings) contain a very much less amount of such surplus binder; unlike oil paint, the bulk of the paint—the water—evaporates completely on drying, leaving the pigment particles exposed or partially exposed to the air. This not only causes the mat effect and the brightness of the hues, but also eliminates a good many of the troublesome ills to which improperly painted oil paintings are subject. It makes necessary a different set of precautions as to the durability of the works, because they are inherently less resistant to wear and tear or to atmospheric conditions; yet many of the oldest paintings in our museums, from the earliest periods, were painted in water techniques.

Regarding permanence, they can be said to be more fragile but just as permanent as oils if properly preserved. For example, water colors are framed under glass and backed with rigid cardboards (or mounted on them), whereas oil paintings are normally framed without glass. Some of the aqueous painting techniques have a considerable degree of material flexibility, but none are so elastic as oils and are therefore not suitable for use on canvas.

The principal difference between the handling or brushing out of water paints and that of oil paints is the more limited special brushwork necessary for using water paints because of their extremely rapid rate of drying as compared with the slow-drying or more plastic oil paints. This narrows the working or manipulative properties of water mediums, and limits the brush work either to free, fresh stroking or to more complex methods, such as allowing the paint to dry and then going over it with other manipulations. However, water color and gouache can be used in blended, graduated and wash effects much more successfully than tempera or fresco, whose handling is in general confined to pencil-like touches applied in single strokes and left alone. Oil paints are the most versatile of all.

Status of water-color painting. It may be noted that water color and gouache are sometimes considered minor techniques when compared with oil painting. This is principally because they are used to instruct beginners and children, or because they are popular for use in making sketches and rough notes from which to paint complete pictures in oil. Actually, water-color painting is as difficult to master as any other technique. Although its effects are more limited than those of oil, they have a distinct appeal of their own, and the process is sufficiently flexible and adaptable to a wide enough range of effects so that it qualifies as a true fine arts medium. It occupies a serious and important place in present-day easel painting.

POSTER COLORS

The water paints sold in glass jars are made by grinding pigments with simple water-soluble binders such as glue, casein, or dextrin, and they contain ordinarily considerable amounts of inert pigment or extender for they are essentially cheap products. A preservative, an odorant and, in some of the better grades, a little glycerin round out the recipes.

Because poster colors are not permanent enough for use in carefully controlled fine arts techniques, they have received scant attention in the books on painting materials. They are widely employed for use in scenery painting, sketching, for purposes of commercial art, illustration and display, and to a considerable extent in educational work. Although poster colors are definitely inferior products from the viewpoint of the accepted, permanent fine-arts paints, they are entirely adequate for the purposes for which they are intended and usually fulfill their own requirements well. The user will note a difference in quality and performance between the cheaper and the more expensive brands. The inert pigments which they all contain are not used solely as cheapeners—such paints requiring a certain amount of bulk in relation to tinting strength —but the cheaper grades will always contain larger amounts of these fillers than the better ones. The distinctions implied in the names given to them by various makers are unstandardized and not indicative of quality. Poster colors, show-card colors, opaque water colors, designers' colors and tempera colors are some of the names by which these products are sold; the last, however, is a misnomer.

Requirements for school use. For school and children's use in general, all dangerously poisonous pigments are excluded from the palette. The following pigments should be strictly forbidden:

Lead pigments—White lead (includes flake and Cremnitz whites).
Naples yellow.
Chrome yellow, orange, and green (including all yellows and greens with common or fancy names not specifically identified in the lists of approved colors for professional artists' use).
Arsenic pigments—Emerald green (Paris green).
Cobalt violet.

These same pigments should also be strictly avoided in pastels and for use in any other method where their dust is liable to be breathed or swallowed. The poisonous colors in liquid paints are not dangerous when handled with a normal degree of care and cleanliness by adults.

Selection of school colors. The author suggests that the list be restricted to the regularly accepted artists' palette, so that the beginners' training in the mixing and handling of color will promote familiarity with the materials they will encounter in advanced work. To this end, the fancy or brilliant aniline colors and imitation pigments should be avoided; they are made for sign, display and decorative work and not intended for general artistic or pictorial use. Handling of the more brilliant aniline colors used in art work designed solely for reproduction can easily be mastered later by the student whose training is based on manipulation of the more subdued permanent colors; habitual reliance on the brilliant lakes and toners at the start will only be harmful to the future production of permanent pictures in the field of creative art. Standard pigment nomenclature ought to be used in place of the fantastic names or simple hue designations often employed.

Recommended palette for school poster colors. The first six pigments in the following list constitute a basic, elementary palette; the rest are listed in order of their general usefulness and value. Individual preferences will vary, however, and selections made according to an instructor's preferences and opinions can very well alter their positions on this list. A full palette of 12 or 14 colors will not always be called for, since that is about the average of the professional artists' palette. The list follows:

Black: Ivory black, lampblack, drop black or Mars black.
White: Zinc or titanium white.
Earth yellow: Ochre, raw sienna, or Mars yellow.
Earth red: Indian red, English red, or burnt sienna.
Bright reds: Cadmium-barium red, light.
              Alizarin red.
Blue: Ultramarine blue.
Green: Viridian or phthalocyanine green.
Bright yellows: Cadmium-barium yellow, medium (golden).
                Cadmium-barium yellow, pale (lemon).
Brown: Burnt umber or raw umber.

Making school colors. Because of its educational value, as an economic measure, or for some other reason, it is occasionally desirable to make some or all of the paints used in school work. The following notes on binding vehicles will be found useful for this purpose. Manufacturers of poster colors alter the proportion and composition of their vehicles to suit the requirements of each pigment, and a manufacturer's recipes may show completely different materials and proportions for different colors. However, this is, in general, too fine a point for amateur paint-grinders to consider.

The binding-vehicle requirements are somewhat different in nature from those which govern the making of fine paints for professional artists' use; permanence, working and visual qualities, etc., are subordinated to economy, ease of mixing and handling, and other factors. As a general rule, home-made poster colors will be found adequate, but they seldom will equal the quality of the best commercially made products unless a considerable amount of care and study goes into their preparation.

All home-made products must be tested to see if they work satisfactorily; therefore, after the colors are made, they are examined to see if the proportion of pigment and adhesive is correct. When painted out on paper in the usual way, the color should not rub or dust off easily; on the other hand, the layer should not be so hard and brittle that it will crack. If the binder is too strong, more pigment and some water are added; if too weak, a stronger or more concentrated binder is used.

For this type of paint, rather generous additions of precipitated chalk or other fillers or inert pigments are allowed and in the case of school colors this means that genuine, full-strength pigments can be used, since even with the more expensive colors the difference in cost between making a paint with them or with cheap substitute colors will seldom be an important consideration. It is not essential that pigments be of the ultimate degree of quality, brilliance and strength—but if they are genuine, they will afford a better introduction to the later use of artists' grade painting materials than the imitation or synthetic colors.

It will be found that Mars black is easier to mix into the water mediums than the other black pigments and, in most cases, will give a sufficiently intense color; its grain, however, is coarser than that of ivory black.

A binding solution made by dissolving white dextrin in boiling hot water to a creamy consistency will be found satisfactory for most poster and school paints. If circumstances warrant it, the more professional gouache or gum tempera binder can be used. In the case of paints for scenery and other large-scale decoration, a simple glue-size solution is customarily employed.

Fine grinding is usually unnecessary; the pigment, with its addition of precipitated chalk (or other inert pigment), is simply stirred to a smooth paste or batter consistency with the white dextrin or glue solution. A little preservative or mold preventive is then added and also perhaps a few drops of oil of cloves or other odorant.

Preservatives and odorants. The following mold preventives or preservatives are efficient for use in aqueous paints:

Small amounts of a weak solution of phenol (carbolic acid) about a half teaspoon of the 1 per cent solution to a pint. Drug stores will generally sell it up to about a 5 per cent solution, this low concentration being deemed harmless.

Sodium orthophenylphenate (trade mark "Dowicide A")—a powder obtainable in chemical supply stores. Small amounts ($\frac{1}{4}$ teaspoon to a quart of binding solution) will effectively preserve gums, casein and glues.

Another older but effective preservative for gum solutions is beta-naphthol used in small amounts.

A 4 per cent solution of formaldehyde. Formaldehyde is likely to react erratically with some binders and is better suited to industrial than amateur use.

The odor of water paints is sometimes a little disagreeable; a *few drops* of any pleasant odorant will correct it. Care must be taken not to perfume the product too strongly, for that will usually be more objectionable than the natural smell of the paint. A "clean-smelling" material such as oil of cloves or sassafras is usually preferred to sweet or flowery odors. Oil of cloves also has a mild preservative action.

Chapter 8

PASTEL

Pastel painting is a completely acceptable, traditional method of creating permanent works of art, and is suitable or adaptable to a wide range of artistic purposes. Depending upon how the technique is handled, pastel is equally effective both for free, spontaneous work and for studied, carefully worked paintings. Bold, powerful strokes, velvety, blended textures, and hard, precise effects—all are within its range. Its color effect is closer to that of the natural dry pigments than that of any other process.

Because no fluid medium or vehicle is used, the method appeals to many painters who find their requirements met by its visual effects without any of the troublesome factors whch sometimes accompany the use of oil or water paints. There is nothing present which is liable to change color, crack, peel or blister, and the final effect is produced immediately without any waits or delays. Also, interruption of work has no technical effect on the process; incomplete paintings may be laid aside and finished at any time.

Pastel is a permanent medium, but the loose, powdery colors on paper are fragile; they demand framing under glass, continual maintainance of normal conditions for preservation, and avoidance of any drastic treatment. The two-century-old portraits which introduced pastel to the art world as a serious fine-arts medium are as fresh today as when they were painted.

In the preservation of any kind of painting, mildew is an enemy to be combatted, but it is more serious in the case of pastel because it is more difficult to remove from the delicate surfaces than from less fragile materials of other works of art. Infestation and growth of mildew on pastel paper and colors may be prevented if a small amount of mold preventive is added to them during their preparation.

Basic principles. In the opening section on page 5, the basic principles which apply to the functioning of the various methods for making permanent paintings were mentioned.

Fig. 58. Normal pastel painting: Left, on fibrous paper; right: on grained paper. (Photomicrographs.)

There pastel was referred to as the simplest, being the application of pure pigment to a surface. Its adhesion is the mechanical gripping or holding of the pigment particles by the roughness or irregularities of the surface. When any crayon, pencil, or similar implement is drawn across the right kind of surface, the action of the surface is like that of a file; the stick is filed down by the rough texture of the ground, and the particles are firmly held in its interstices (see Figure 55). Among the various papers and boards available to the artist for use with any sort of pencil, crayon or pastel, there are just two varieties from the pastel standpoint: one will attract and hold pigment particles, the other will repel them or allow them to fall away. This difference is to be found in all types of surfaces—smooth, rough or granular—so that any new kind of paper has to be tried before using.

The sticks or crayons of artists' fine pastels are soft although harder pastels are sometimes used for special effects. They contain just enough of a weak gum solution to hold them together in crayon shape and allow them to be used in a free manner without excessive breaking or crumbling if handled in a reasonably skillful manner. This small amount of binder has no effect on the colors or the picture but it does give the particles sufficient cohesion to permit the color to be piled up to a slight impasto (Figure 58). Pastel colors cannot be heaped on too thickly or indiscriminately and remain permanently attached to the surface but neither do they have to be extremely smooth or evenly applied unless the individual painter wishes them to be so by choice. It is this slight variation in texture and thickness of layer which produces effects with appeal for many painters.

Pastel grounds. There are two main kinds of pastel paper or board in general use: one has the normal coarse, rough, irregular grain of unpressed water-color or drawing paper (see page 155) on which the particles of color are held by the paper fibers; the other is a type of specially prepared pastel surface which has a tooth (a granular roughness similar to extremely fine sandpaper) produced by applying a special coating to a permanent paper or board. The two kinds are roughly equal in popularity. The granular sort is, in general, more versatile as it is best adapted to the smooth, blended type of work; however, the fibrous or ordinary rough drawing paper type is not technically inferior, and is often preferred for its textural qualities.

Pastel papers are often sold colored, or they may be painted on with water color before the crayons are used. If a solid, all-over pastel painting is made, the color of the ground has very little effect because, unlike fluid paints, the pastel pigments have a total hiding power. If the color is applied sparingly, with areas of the ground left visible, great advantage can be taken of a colored paper or an underpainting in water color.

The impossibility of transparent color effect or of glazing has been cited as being the only technical shortcoming of pastel as compared with the fluid mediums.

Fixatives. Pastel paintings can be made somewhat more durable, as regard handling and rubbing, by spraying them with one of the prepared fixatives which are sold for the purpose. These are usually very weak spirit varnishes—solutions of about 2 per cent of some resin in alcohol. However, almost every artist who specializes in pastel from a serious or professional standpoint dislikes the use of fixatives because of the inevitable change they make in the color and textural effect. As previously mentioned on page 23, the surrounding of pigment particles with a substance of different refractive index must, in conformance with an optical law, vary its color effect; and because no two pigments will be altered to the same degree, the color changes produced in fixing a pastel is often quite disappointing. Textural effect is also altered by a sort of hardening or tightening of contours, because of the fusion of particles in the liquid.

Despite a two hundred years' search for a satisfactory means of fixing pastels, the experienced, professional users of pastel still prefer unfixed or very slightly fixed paintings, preserved by framing securely under glass.

Mounting, transporting and handling. Although pastel pictures can be smeared badly if rubbed, they will stand a limited amount of careful, steady direct pressure against shiny surfaces, such as glossy coated paper and cellophane. By exercising the proper degree of caution, and avoiding any lateral or rubbing movement, pastels may be mounted, packed, and transported as are water colors.

Pastel as a medium for sketches and notes. Pastel competes with water color as a sketch medium; an easily portable, compact outfit may consist of a small, flat box of pastels and a supply of granular pastel paper carried within the leaves of a glossy paper booklet or magazine.

Sanitary precautions. One must avoid the continuous inhalation of the dusty powder which is likely to arise from the normal application of pastels to the paper, as well as from rubbing or manipulating them. It is well known that no dusty powders (ordinary talcum powder, for example) should be inhaled. Harmless though their nature may be, the continued breathing of any powders is injurious to health. For this reason, pastels are not ideal materials for young children's use, nor for individuals who may be oversensitive or allergic to such powders.

The few definitely poisonous pigments are—or should be—strictly excluded from the pastel palette. The principal ones to avoid are as follows:

The lead pigments (which are also not reliably permanent for pastel use). White lead (flake and Cremnitz whites). Naples yellow, chrome yellows, and chrome greens.

The arsenic pigments. Cobalt violet, and emerald green.

With the observance of normal precautions against swallowing or breathing these materials, these pigments are perfectly safe in liquid paints for adult use, but none of them should be employed in pastels.

Home-made pastels. Pastels may be listed among the artists' materials which can be home-made to advantage. The artist is rewarded for the time spent on this simple and easy process by obtaining a supply of good, practical materials at a small fraction of the cost of ready-made crayons. There are certain other advantages, which the pastels of the shops unfortunately do not always possess, that the ready-made product has; one is assured that permanent pigments are used, that the sticks have the right degree of hardness or softness, and any favorite shade, tint or mixture of colors can be made. No elaborate apparatus is needed for home-made pastels, Figure 59 showing all the necessary materials.

The traditional binder is gum tragacanth; a modern substitute is methyl cellulose. One-half ounce of the material is allowed to soak in 24 ounces of water overnight in a warm

place, and the resulting gelatinous mass is then shaken or
stirred to a homogeneous consistency: a portion of this is
diluted with an equal amount of water, another portion with
three parts of water and these binders in three different
strengths are used to mix with the dry pigments (Figure 60) to

FIG. 59. Group of materials used in making pastel crayons.

make a stiff dough. From this dough the crayons are rolled out
on sheets of newspaper and allowed to dry at normal room
temperature (Figure 62). If it is desired to store the gum-
tragacanth solutions, $\frac{1}{8}$ to $\frac{1}{4}$ teaspoon of beta-naphthol added
to it during its making will insure its keeping for years in well-
corked bottles. The methyl cellulose requires no preservative.*
The reason for the three different solutions is that each pig-

* These solutions are somewhat weaker than those suggested by the author
in *The Artist's Handbook* and they constitute an improvement over the old
measurement.

ment has a different binding strength when mixed with water; thus it is necessary to do a little experimental or trial mixing of small test pieces to determine the best mixture for making crayons which combine *softness* of texture with adequate *crayon strength*. If the solution is too strong, or too weak, the pastels will be deficient in one of those two requirements. For ex-

FIG. 60. Pastel crayons: Mixing pigment and binder.

ample, alizarin red usually requires a strong solution, burnt sienna a middle-strength solution, and raw umber a very weak solution. Viridian usually has such strong binding properties by itself that even plain water will make pastels which are too hard, and a mixture of three parts of alcohol to one of water has to be used. Commercially made pastels contain a variety of binders and modifying ingredients to improve the properties and overcome the shortcomings of various pigments.

In addition to the full-strength colors and mixtures of colors, the artist will require a full scale of tints or reductions with white for each color. These are made, according to correct steps of equal visual ratios, by dividing the full strength pastel dough into two equal parts (Figure 63) and, after rolling crayons out of one of these parts, thoroughly mixing the other part with an equal volume of white dough made of precipitated chalk and binding solution (Figures 64 and 65). The mass is then divided again into two equal parts and the process repeated, rolling crayons out of one part and mixing the remain-

FIG. 61. Pastel crayons: Proper consistency of the dough.

ing part with an equal amount of white dough. After repeating this procedure several times, the end of the series is reached when the tints are so pale that any further reduction with white will not produce useful shades. From five to eight or more tints can be made depending on the tinting strength of the pigment.

The dough must always be mixed to the most convenient, stiff putty consistency, so that it can be neatly rolled to a ball between the palms without either stickiness or crumbling (Figure 61). Slight differences are adjusted by adding a few drops of water or a little chalk. Simple finger rolling (Figure

62) makes crayons satisfactory to most painters; smoother ones can be made by rolling with a small board instead of with the fingers. The inexpensive aluminum cake decorator (Figure 59) is considered practical by some people and an unnecessary gadget by others. The old telephone book is as good as newspapers for many such operations and is also a handy rag-saver about the studio.

FIG. 62. Pastel crayons: Rolling the dough into crayon shape.

Definite, measured recipes or proportions for binder and pigment cannot always be relied on because of the great variations in raw materials from different sources. The artist should keep an accurate and permanent record of his mixtures, so that they can be duplicated in subsequent batches made from gum and pigments having the same sources. Pure precipitated chalk is the customary white pigment used for white and pale tints of pastels. When measuring dry powders, care is taken to prevent packing them into the measure, otherwise the results will be erratic and irregular. The careful worker pours the powder loosely into the measure and levels it off gently. (Figure 66.)

FIG. 63. Pastel crayons: Dividing the batch in half by approximation.

FIG. 64. Pastel crayons: An accurate way to measure the tints.

FIG. 65. Some makers prefer to mix tints in a mortar and pestle instead of with a spatula.

FIG. 66. Leveling a measure of dry powder accurately without packing it in.

Chapter 9

MURAL PAINTING

Compared with easel painting. Mural painting is a branch of art distinct from easel painting, because the decoration of walls imposes upon the painter a set of physical, technical and artistic requirements different from those he is called upon to fulfill when he paints an easel picture in his studio, or a landscape outdoors, or any kind of readily portable painting.

An easel painting is a separate unit, an autonomous work of art. It is meant to go within the confining limits of a picture frame; and although it is ordinarily hung on a wall with care and some consideration for its decorative value, it is also placed where the spectator can view it from one selected, fixed point, under the best special lighting permitted by circumstances. A mural painting must be effective when viewed at any angle from any point in the room. Ideally, a mural painting is supposed to be a permanent and integral part of the architecture, a part of the building rather than a superimposed embellishment such as a framed easel painting. A mural for a new or proposed building must be planned in full co-ordination with the design and function of the room; for an existing structure it must be planned so that it seems to belong there, and its design must be subordinated to that of its surroundings. Appropriateness of choice must be considered even more carefully than in easel painting, and it is essential to avoid "the application of inappropriate materials to alien surfaces and surroundings."

Requirements. The technical requirements of a mural process are:

The careful preparation of the wall is the first and most important consideration in fresco painting. The first coarse or rough coat of plaster is carefully laid on a perfectly sound brick or masonry wall; in modern construction, sometimes on metal lath. Then two coats of progressively finer-textured plaster are applied, and finally the pure white painting surface which is the finest in texture. Each of these coats is most meticulously proportioned; carefully prepared, selected ingredients are used, and they must be trowelled in a skilled, experienced manner. An outline of the design of the mural is traced onto the wall after the last undercoat has dried, and the final painting ground of white plaster is laid over this drawing in sections. Only an area which can be painted in one day is covered each time, since the painting can be done only on the wet, fresh surface.

The chemical principle of fresco depends on some of the simple basic reactions of everyday chemistry. Quicklime (calcium oxide, CaO) is slaked or mixed with water, which produces hydrated lime $Ca(OH)_2$, and this is aged until it attains a plastic consistency called lime putty. The mortars for the various coats are made by mixing this with the proper amounts of sand and marble grit, which prevents shrinkage of the mass.

Fresco is a process in which the sole function of the vehicle (pure water) is to put the color into fluid form so that it can be thinly and transparently applied to the wet wall surface; the wall itself supplies the binding action as it dries and sets.

The pigments are drawn into the wall surface by capillary action and are securely bound with it; the binding action is no more or less than the binding or cementing action of the plaster particles on each other and on the sand and marble grit. They are not surrounded or encased by a vehicle, but are exposed to the atmosphere; hence they must be carefully selected from among the most chemically inert colors. Besides having to be proof against the powerfully alkaline action of the lime, the pigments must also resist the acid impurities of the atmosphere. The fresco palette is more strictly limited than that of any of our other methods.

More detailed accounts of fresco and secco will be found in the books listed on page 211. Practical fresco painting may be learned by apprenticeship, and by instruction, supplemented by individual trials. Written accounts of fresco will give less of an understanding of its control than is the case with any other among all the various painting processes, unless it is supplemented by actual, first-hand experience with the materials and their application.

The mural painter does not begin the painting stage of his work until he is certain his materials are under control, and even the experienced worker usually has a few tests going on while the preliminary arrangements of a job are being made. New pigments do not always perform in the same way as a previously used lot; a pigment may require additional binder or a different type binder on various surfaces. Nevertheless, there are many details and problems which arise after the painting has started; only the experienced mural painter can cope with these.

OTHER MURAL METHODS

Secco. Another process about which there are written records dating from the earliest European sources, and relics from still earlier times, is known as secco or limewash painting. In modern times it is generally considered a good second-choice method to be used in circumstances where fresco is impractical. Unlike fresco it can be painted on a finished, completely dry lime-plaster wall of any age. However, a pure lime-plaster wall is required, the more common gypsum or magnesian plasters being unsuitable. In this process the water-ground pigments are usually mixed with an aqueous binding medium and the result is a superficial surface coating, like any other paint. Yet its effect is closer to true fresco than any of the other processes, and its handling requires much the same method of execution.

The process. At night, the clean, lime-plaster wall is drenched with as much limewater (solution of quicklime in cold distilled water) as the wall will absorb, and in the morning it is again soaked thoroughly with limewater. The water-ground colors—the same permanent ones as those used in fresco painting—are mixed with an equal volume of binding medium which can be either a strong solution of hide-glue, or casein, or pure egg yolk. A little prior experimenting is necessary to determine the desirable strength of the binding medium because of variations in conditions. The wall is kept moist during painting by spraying with more limewater. Painting strokes and manipulations are the same as with fresco painting; plenty of water must be added, and the paint must be thinly used in a transparent or translucent manner, not piled up in impasto. Although casein is hardened by the action of the limewater, the work is usually not sufficiently water-resistant to be cleaned by water and requires the same cleaning method as does tempera (page 151).

Many variations of detail have been developed through the years and in different localities, and numerous personal preferences exist among painters as to details. Another secco method employs *limewash* (a much-diluted lime putty) applied to a coarse plaster wall in several coats with a calcimine brush.

The variations encountered in the binding requirements of the various pigments in water mediums have already been mentioned; in secco painting one must be particularly certain that each color is going to be well attached to the wall. All the aqueous binding materials, glue, casein, egg, etc., have been mentioned from the earliest writings down to the work of modern instructors. Some painters mix limewater with the pigments; this naturally gives them a paler color when dry. The processes outlined here are typical but by no means the only methods used or recommended by experts.

The word *secco* has also been used in another sense, meaning simply dry, or painting on dry walls as distinguished from painting on wet walls in true fresco. Cennini, for example, used the term to describe the finishing or retouching of dried frescoes with tempera paints, using pigments ground either in egg yolk or whole egg mixed with fig tree juice.

Tempera on walls. Much of the desirable visual effect of fresco painting can be approximated by the use of tempera paints directly on a dry plaster wall (any well-plastered surface, not necessarily pure lime-plaster). The paint is thinly applied in the fresco manner so as to produce a smooth, level, uniform surface. Tempera murals can be cleaned by sponging or swabbing with absorbent cotton moistened with acetone or anhydrous alcohol, as they are not sufficiently moisture-proof to withstand periodic cleaning with water.

Murals in oil. Oil-painting techniques, although admirably suited to the production of easel paintings, give results which are inferior to all the other mural processes when applied to walls, because they meet so few of the mural requirements. However, because of various circumstances, murals are often painted in oil; there are three principal ways in which this is done, as follows:

1. Straight oil painting on primed, plaster walls.
2. Imitations of fresco and other processes.
3. Paintings done in the studio on canvas and then cemented to the walls. The traditional cement for this purpose is commercial white lead in oil, mixed with a little varnish to give it a tacky or sticky consistency. The cementing process is known as mural hanging, and is sometimes called by its French name *marouflage*.

The use of oil paints falls short of the requirements of a mural process, as listed previously, especially as to permanence and optical effects. When oil paintings become discolored, dilapidated or blemished, they require expert, skilled conservation treatments in order to recondition them, and most of these have to be done carefully by professional restorers. Even simple cleaning and revarnishing of an oil painting become extremely difficult when attempted on a painting that cannot be removed from the wall and laid flat. On walls and especially where canvas grounds are used, oil paint attracts dirt and grime and holds it tenaciously to the surface. The glossy or irregularly mat and glossy areas are far below the water mediums

in visual effectiveness. Oil painting on walls is best confined to
work of minor artistic importance; lesser decorative painting
that is intended to be replaced after a limited period. Frequent
dusting is necessary to prevent the rapid accumulation of dirt.

Murals to resist especially drastic conditions. For outdoor
urban exposure or in places where very severe conditions exist,
none of the foregoing traditional processes is recommended; if
absolute permanence is required, some special method is usually devised to meet the circumstances. Among these methods
may be mentioned the use of mosaic, painted and fired terra-
cotta tiles, porcelain enameling on iron sheets, carved bas-relief
in stone painted in flat colors that can be replaced when worn
or discolored, and integrally colored Portland cement. Another
possibility lies in the fresco-like results obtained from some of
our modern synthetic materials which are at present in the
development or experimental stage, notably the use of ethyl
silicate and the silicones.

ENCAUSTIC

Encaustic is a method of easel or mural painting, on any
ground or surface, with paints made by simply mixing dry pigments with molten, white refined beeswax. One of the oldest
of painting techniques, it was used extensively in ancient
Greece, and the surviving Fayoum portraits from Egypt done
in the second century attest to its permanence. Fluently executed portraits have survived, strikingly fresh and brilliant,
when preserved under conditions which have protected them
against mechanical wear and tear.

The usual method is to place the wax colors on a warm
palette, then paint directly on a warmed surface with brushes
and heat-resistant, spatulate implements. The strokes can be
worked over, refined, and smoothed with warm implements;
if ground and palette can be kept within the proper range of
temperature (not too hot and not too cool), fluent and easy
painting can be done in a direct, fresh manner. The word
encaustic means "burning in" and most methods call for a

warming of the surface after the colors have been applied, in order to fuse them.

The brilliance, color, and textural effects are quite distinctive and lend themselves well to several modern tendencies in art; this accounts for a small but growing, present-day revival of interest in this ancient method.

Encaustic became a lost art at the time when the kind of picture in demand was the egg tempera type and it never regained its popularity as an art-medium because of the cumbersome and unwieldly equipment required in the days when charcoal fires were used as the sources of heat. By adapting modern electric heating units to the purpose, it is possible to improvise reasonably simple arrangements by which the correct warm temperature of paints and ground can be maintained and the work done easily and without complications.

Wax, as previously mentioned, is one of our most permanent and chemically inert binding materials, but its film is more tender than that of an oil painting and must be preserved against wear and scratching. The effect of a robust and full-bodied paint quality can be obtained without much actual heavy impasto, with smooth films of wax colors. If polished with a soft cloth, the surface takes on a pleasing dull sheen, and such a surface repels dust better than oil paint. Most investigators of this traditional or "classic" method, recommend melting in varying amounts of resin with the wax to increase hardness.

Wax color is a cleanly material to handle; palettes, vessels and instruments may be quickly and thoroughly cleaned by warming them and wiping off the color with a cloth. The brushes do not have to be kept spotlessly clean if each one is reserved for a separate color. Care must be taken not to overheat or singe the bristles. One can go through the entire procedure without the use of solvents; when a solvent is necessary, carbon tetrachloride is the best.

Many variations and modifications of the traditional encaustic process have been proposed by artists and by students of old techniques. Some of these have been presented as authentic versions of the original methods and others as inventions or improvements. Oils and resins have been mixed with the wax, wax soap or emulsified waxes have been recommended, but none of these procedures is founded on completely reliable historical data. During an eighteenth century revival of encaustic, a proposed method was advanced which gave quite interesting results. This method consisted in warming the surface of a canvas or panel and then coating it by rubbing it with a cake of white beeswax. The surface is dusted over with dry chalk, and the picture painted with pigments ground in plain water—the chalk permitting the water colors to take on the waxy surface. The colors are allowed to dry, and then the work is brought near enough to a heat source to soften the wax (either by moving the picture or the heating unit), whereupon the softened wax will surround the pigment particles, bringing out their full color value and encasing them in a protective film of wax. If a horizontal position is maintained (either face up or face down) the wax colors will not run unless grossly overheated. The surface is more tender and subject to damage than that produced by applying pigmented wax to the surface. Another variation was to paint on linen with water-vehicle colors, coat the rear with beswax and drive the wax through the canvas with a warm iron so that the colors become impregnated with it.

In mixing wax (or wax plus resin) paints for the usual or "classic" method, one of the principal points to be kept in mind is the proportion between pigment and wax—which, like pigment and oil, varies with each pigment. If there is too much pigment, the warm paint will not remain fluid long enough to give satisfactory brushing qualities; if there is too much wax, the finished paint will be tender and will not resist the softening effect of a warm climate the way well-proportioned wax colors do to a remarkable degree.

All the pigments listed under the permanent oil painting palette on page 35 may be used in encaustic. At the present time, the practice of encaustic painting is hampered by the lack of reliable published data on its details, and some well-directed systematic research toward this end would be a welcome addition to our fund of information on painting techniques. Until then, encaustic will continue to demand a certain amount of experiment by the painter.

Chapter 10

STUDIO AND EQUIPMENT

There are a number of elementary, basic procedures, conventions and habits which an artist acquires in a casual or accidental way on entering his career. Some of these seem so natural and simple that they are seldom treated as points of instruction, since the artist becomes acquainted with them by observation, by experience and through chats with fellow artists on which occasions such matters have always been favorite subjects of conversation and argument.

Some of the topics discussed in this chapter may appear to be of minor importance, since they refer to the artist's comfort and convenience rather than to the technical problems of paint, but comfort and convenience are by no means minor considerations. Successful work can be and has been done under the most unfavorable surroundings and with the most inadequate equipment; however, painting presents such problems and difficulties under the best of conditions that the first rule on beginning to paint is always to get comfortable and to take advantage of as many physical conveniences as are available.

THE STUDIO

An ideal painting room has always been designed with a north light and with an absence or minimum of outdoor obstructions. The light from the north is steadier, more constant and less glaring throughout the day; eastern exposure is second best because the glare diminishes early in the day. However, some painters do not object to their light being glaring and changeable; they seem to be able to get along under conditions which would be intolerable to others.

Studio windows are large because the average painter requires a large area of his room to be evenly illuminated, not just a little spot. They are large because he wants *intensity* of light as well as quality and because it requires a large area of window surface to illuminate the painting area on dull days and late afternoons. The argument over the advantages of overhead skylights versus side windows has been going on for many years and it seems to be a matter of personal preference or to depend on the type of work being done. However, a skylight is most desirable when a studio is adjacent to taller buildings or other obstructions to light. Reflections from buildings and objects which color the light or from window panes which reflect the sun can be quite annoying.

Most of us who work with color believe that artificial light —including the daylight lamps with special lenses or fluorescent lights—no matter how successfully it imitates the quality of daylight is a substitute or makeshift arrangement to be used only when circumstances prevent the use of daylight. However other artists and many optical and scientific experts tell us this is prejudice and that modern equipment has standardized lighting to such a degree that, because of its uniformity and control of color quality, artificial light actually creates working conditions more efficient than the variable circumstances supplied by nature. The chief deficiencies some artists find in artificial studio lighting are the glare and the lack of intensity. The psychological element may also enter into it, but the majority of painters find that they are happier and more comfortable working in daylight.

Although he frequently makes an effort to create an atmosphere of taste and comfort in his studio, the modern earnest professional painter is more likely to be found in a rather bare, utilitarian workshop, free from both the disorderly clutter or the salon-like over-decoration of the recent past. His tools and equipment are well cared for, kept under cover as much as possible and the room is arranged so that it can be periodically cleaned without disturbance.

Dust. The combination of dust, soot and fog which envelops large towns and cities is a condition with which the painter has long contended. At some future date he may inhabit completely air-conditioned rooms, but at present dust and soot are more a bugaboo than ever, and each painter must work out his own arrangements for their control.

Ventilation. The dust menace is also complicated by the need for ventilation beyond the normal necessity for indoor work, especially because the presence of vapors from volatile solvents, dust from powdered pigments or pastels, and odors from paint make a continuous supply of fresh air essential.

Privacy. Whenever possible, the painting room should have provisions for maintaining privacy. Although the artist may not object to having company while at work and may not be concerned about being occasionally interrupted, he usually finds that eventually there come times when intruders and distracting movements must be shut out; and so, in choosing a painting space, an arrangement that permits the enforcement of privacy is desirable.

IMPLEMENTS AND EQUIPMENT

Brushes. The brushes used by the artist are sensitive tools, the products of a highly developed craft whose history is as long as that of the colors and paints he uses. They are more than just little bundles of hairs or bristles stuck into metal ferrules or quills and attached to wooden handles. The making of best quality brushes, both for artists' and for housepainters' use, is an art which involves highly skilled manual operations as well as the selection of superlative materials. Hence, they can be obtained only from a limited number of sources, and the procurement of good brushes is generally one of the painters' first concerns. Like the instruments or tools of any craft, those of highest quality will give superior results, and if not abused they will outlast the inferior kinds and make their initial expense a worthwhile investment.

The painter must not stint himself on either quality or quantity. He should never buy a poor brush and whenever he has the opportunity to buy a few fine ones, he should do so, even if it limits his purchases of other supplies; he should try to accumulate dozens of them. Very often, a brush that has been broken in by use and proper care, will suit the artist better than a new one; if he has plenty in use and new ones in reserve his favorites will not wear out too soon. If he has all types and sizes on hand he will always have the one most sympathetic to his purposes when he needs it.

For normal use in all our accepted methods of painting, both bristle brushes and the softer hair brushes should possess a liveliness or springiness which the cheaper brushes usually lack. Their shapes should be symmetrical; the round ones should come to a fine point and the flat ones to an even edge. The careful purchaser tests these qualities by examining them closely.

The point of a brush is never cut or trimmed; the exposed ends are the natural tips of the hairs or bristles and the shaping of a brush is done by careful setting of the opposite ends during its manufacture. The hairs or bristles used in a good brush are sometimes twice as long as the visible portion that extends out of the metal ferrule.

Bristle brushes. For oil painting, brushes in either round or flat shapes made of bleached hog bristles (Figure 68) are generally used. In order to insure against the outer bristles of the round and the corners of the flat brushes splaying out to an undesirably ragged and uncontrollable fringe, incurving bristles are used. The flat shapes are a comparatively modern innovation; the older painters seldom, if ever, used anything but round ones. Flat brushes are more versatile and convenient, especially with the pastier, less fluid paints preferred by most painters today. Beside the regular flats, a shorter-bristled, thinner variety called "brights" is also in use. There are two number eights in Figure 68, the one on the right side is a bright, the one in the center a flat.

Other shapes in less frequent use are the oval brushes—a flat brush with rounded corners that approximates the appearance of a worn-down flat or bright—and the chisel brushes—flats which are sharply beveled and come to a thin edge.

Sable brushes. For all the water mediums, red sable water-color brushes (Figure 67) are first choice. The so-called camel's-hair brushes and those made from other hairs whose character is limp or less springy than red sable are less suitable for normal water-color painting, but they have their occasional uses for various effects and preferences. Red sable brushes are also used for oil painting, especially for smoother, blended or less vigorous stroking; these are ordinarily made with shorter hairs and longer handles than the water-color brushes and are obtainable in both round and flat shapes (Figure 69). The kind called "flats" come to a rather blunt point almost like an oval or worn, flat bristle brush, and the kind called "brights" have more sharply squared edges.

Few handicraft products are uniform, and water-color brushes are no exception; the purchaser will find that while all the brushes in a lot of highest quality are acceptable, individual ones will vary slightly in sharpness of point, symmetry of form, etc. In the case of the round, pointed brushes, it is customary for the artist to try out a few of the size he wants and using the container of water the dealer usually has on his counter for the purpose, moisten them, shake them out and examine the point, the shape and the resiliency in order to select the ones best suited to his purposes.

As a rule, first-class bristle brushes for oil painting run more uniform and there is less choice between the individual brushes in a lot; their quality can be best judged after they have been put into use. In selecting them, one ordinarily depends on the brand name and the dealer's information. It should be noted that new brushes often have a bit of starch in them in order to keep their shapes from being distorted or damaged in

FIG. 69. Red sable oil-painting brushes.

FIG. 68. Bristle brushes.

FIG. 67. Red sable water-color brushes.

handling, and so, in the shop, the inferior ones may be as good-
looking as the fine ones.

Although the finest brushes for artists are usually well finished—their handles and metal ferrules showing evidence of
high quality and workmanship—brushes cannot always be

FIG. 70. Badger brush.

judged by their finish. Sometimes fine brushes will be found
with very simple handles whereas sometimes the handles of
poor brushes are attractively polished. Some brushes are set
in the old-fashioned manner in quills instead of in metal ferrules; these require mounting on pointed wooden sticks which
are supplied with them. Quill brushes are not so widely em-

ployed as they were formerly. Very fine red sable, as well as more commonplace grades, are made.

Other brushes. A perusal of the brush section of an artists' material catalog or the examination of a dealer's stock will reveal the existence of a huge number of special-purpose brushes, some of which are extremely useful, although they may have been designed for use in other crafts or for artists' manipulations which were more popular in bygone days. Among these are the *badger blender* (Figure 70) which is meant for softening or "sweetening" the gradation between two areas of different shades or hues. It resembles a shaving brush and is intended to be used dry and clean with a vertical, up-and-down pouncing or tapping motion on wet paint, the painting being laid flat on a table. The texture produced is very smooth or else finely stippled. *Riggers* (Figure 71A) are springy red sable round lettering brushes with blunt ends and usually rather long hairs. The small sizes are useful for thin lines. In America the name also refers to the size and proportion of this particular type of brush. *Single-stroke lettering brushes* (Figure 71B) are made in flat shapes of red sable, ox-hair or a blend of the two, and many water-color painters find the wide ones invaluable for all sorts of manipulations. The fan brushes, both bristle and sable (Figure 71C) are used to sweep wet paint into wispy effects; for delicate blending, etc.

Varnish brushes. Wide, flat brushes of the types illustrated in Figure 45 (page 126) are the most suitable for varnishing paintings and for applying gesso (page 84); their bristles are long and flexible. The thin types are the best, but when they are not available in good quality, the regular house-painter's varnish brush of thicker construction may be used. The most annoying defect of a varnish brush is shedding of bristles; purchase of an inferior varnish brush is just as false economy as selection of an inferior artists' brush. Stability of bristles, resiliency and symmetry of shape are the characteristics of a good varnish brush.

The careful painter reserves his varnish brushes especially

for varnishing, and when not in use he protects them by wrapping them in paper. They must be kept scrupulously clean, not only for the sake of clean, speck-free varnish, but also be-

FIG. 71. Riggers, Single-stroke, Fans.

cause an accumulation at the base of the bristles will rob the brush of much flexibility and may cause bristles to break at this point. Some painters do not approve of washing them like paint brushes, but simply rinse them repeatedly in small portions of clean turpentine, shaking them out well, and changing the turpentine between each rinsing.

Brush sizes. The sizes of brushes are almost completely standardized; but occasionally, there will be a discrepancy in some imported lines. The numbers assigned to the various sizes however, are not the same for each type of brush, for example a number 12 water-color brush is nothing like a number 12 bristle brush. Some specialty brushes use special numbering, for example, some types of quill brushes are numbered in reverse order, that is, the highest number designates the smallest brush. Another group is named after birds, swan, goose, crow, etc. The single-stroke lettering brush is graded in widths; the one illustrated (Figure 71B) is marked 1".

The tiniest brushes have their uses and are invaluable in specific cases, but in general the artist prefers to use the largest ones he can. He prizes the big ones not only because they are more expensive, but because they give better results, they are usually the mainstay of his work and the smaller ones are supplementary.

Care and cleaning of brushes. There is no point in going to the trouble of selecting fine brushes with care and discrimination unless they are to be treated with the care and respect deserving of such valuable instruments.

As far as is compatible with the purposes of the painter, painting should be done with the forward portion of the brush; no brush including the house painter's, should be continually plunged into the paint up to the ferrule, but the material should be taken up by the front part of the bristles. This not only allows of cleaner, neater, more efficient application, but also makes for longevity of the brush. Paint which works its way into the root of the bristles or hairs and into the ferrule is extremely difficult to remove by ordinary cleaning methods; should the paint dry or become permanently caked there, the full usefulness of the brush is impaired. Of course it is not possible to conform to this rule in all cases, but the careful painter bears it in mind, and tries to avoid unnecessary clogging.

Brushes of all kinds should be wiped, rinsed with turpentine, water or whatever the solvent of the paint or varnish is, shaken out and wiped again as soon as is feasible after use. They are then washed with soap and running warm water, being careful to rinse out all traces of soap. The brushes are then "dressed" (squeezed out between the fingers and pointed), and laid away carefully to dry in a dust-free place.

If time limitations or other considerations make it seem desirable to keep the brushes submerged in turpentine, oil or water in order to keep them moist, care must be taken to have them suspended freely in the liquid so their shapes will not become distorted by coming in contact with the container. Special holders for water-color brushes are sold in the supply stores. For several reasons, long submersion in liquids is not the best way to preserve fine brushes.

Brush terminology. Among the technical terms commonly used in describing the parts of a brush are the following:

The *tip* or *point* is the extreme end of the hairs or bristles. The natural ends of hairs and bristles are split, forked or tapered, and this is called the *flag* (manufacturers sometimes refer to the tip of the brush as flag). The metal in which the brush and its handle is set is called the *ferrule,* and the point where the brushes emerge from the ferrule is usually called the *neck.* The best round water-color brush should have a pronounced bulge about halfway between the ferrule and the point; this is the *belly.* When wet and pointed, little or no concavity should exist between the belly and the point. The round oil-painting sable and bristle brushes do not have bellies; there is just a slightly curved taper from the ferrule to the tip. The *heel* of a brush refers to a shape which it assumes in use, rather than to a part; for example, when a stroke is made with the side of a round bristle brush pressed rather firmly down on the canvas, and the principal point of contact is a firm, springy spot at a small but appreciable distance *away* from the ferrule, it is said to form a heel. A limp, floppy brush will not form a heel. Some painters rely on this sort of action; a rather worn, old brush is likely to have it, although one in which old paint or oil has accumulated at the neck is likely to have too much.

Palette knives. Figure 72 shows a group of the spatulas or palette knives which are essential studio equipment. All these

1   2 3 4 5 6

FIG. 72. Palette Knives.

should be of fine quality, well tempered and springy. The bluntly rounded type, Nos. 2 and 6, are most useful for heavy duties such as mixing pigments with vehicles and handling stiff pastes on the grinding slab; they are also available in many other sizes. The tapered, more limber variety like Nos. 3, 4 and 5, are more suitable for handling or scraping paints on the palette and canvas. No. 1, the broad blade with its edge at the front, is usually called a "wall scraper" in the hardware stores and is the best type of instrument for applying, scraping away or spreading out coatings over large flat areas or for handling larger quantities of paint on the grinding slab. Like the palette knife, it is efficient only if made of best-quality flexible, tempered steel. The cheaper, narrower putty knife of stiff construction, however, also has its uses about the studio.

FIG. 73. Painting knives.

With continual wear, the edges of palette knives will become very sharp, sometimes achieving a razor keenness. This hazardous condition can be avoided by watchfulness and occasionally blunting the sides with a file or whetstone; but when they wear exceedingly thin, they should be replaced.

Painting knives. (Figure 73.) The painting knife is distinguished from the palette knife by its extreme flexibility, springiness and delicacy. Essentially miniature trowel-like implements made in a variety of shapes and sizes, they are intended to be used to deposit and spread oil colors on a painting *and for nothing else.* Painting-knives are or should be sensitive, carefully balanced, fine tempered steel blades; they are quite fragile and easily ruined if not given proper treatment. Although a thin spatulate instrument was used in one form or another by the ancients, especially the bronze *cestrum* used in encaustic painting, our modern delicate painting-knife does not appear to have been used in European painting prior to the middle of the nineteenth century. Careful technicians warn against the use of oil color in excessively thick impasto (see page 131), and the painting knife sometimes tempts one to go too far in this respect. However, when it is thoughtfully and intelligently controlled, the painting knife can be a valuable instrument to secure various textures and effects that cannot easily be duplicated by brush manipulations alone.

Easels. There are many models of easels available; some are so adjustable that they will accommodate the size of the painting, the desired height, etc., without much effort; others are more troublesome. The artist usually tries to obtain the most efficient and complete easel for studio use, and is limited only by his pocketbook in its selection. However, the first consideration in selecting an easel should be its rigidity and stability, since the prime necessity is that it hold the painting in a steady, motionless manner, without wavering or threatening to collapse. The larger models are generally most desirable; this does not necessarily mean that the very heaviest type is the best, but an easel must be in good, tight condition, and designed so as to combine the maximum stability with sufficient adjustability.

Sketching easels. A very wide selection of portable folding easels for outdoor use will be found in the supply shops. Nearly all of them can be considered desirable for some requirement or another because for the most part their designs have been evolved as a result of long experience. However, artists have very strong preferences for certain types, and individuals usually make their selections according to personal requirements and the conditions of use.

Portability, which takes into consideration both size and weight, is balanced against rigidity, stability, simplicity, durability and ease of operation. Experience soon determines the type best suited to the user.

Palettes. The surface on which the painter squeezes out the colors for his day's work and from which he takes them up with his brush to apply to his painting can be anything he chooses. He is not necessarily limited to the traditional oval or oblong thumbhole palette made of a thin hardwood board or any of its variations to be found in the dealer's stocks. He should, rather, select the kind of surface that is best suited to his way of working, the materials or techniques involved, and the circumstances or working conditions.

The regular thumbhole palette, meant to be held in the left hand, serves well in some circumstances, especially when working away from the studio or in a crowded classroom, but for studio use a large percentage of artists prefer to use a flat slab of plate glass, opaque white glass or white marble, placed on a table next to the easel. It permits easier and more rapid color preparation and frees both hands for the work. Smaller pieces of plate glass, china plates and platters, cups, saucers and tins may all be called into use on occasion. The color of the palette is of great concern to some painters; the modern tendency is to use pure white surfaces, and sometimes their hand palettes are lacquered white or some pale, neutral shade which they may prefer.

Painters sometimes become so accustomed to the use of a foul palette that they work with it in preference to a clean one, but this is purely a habit and is to be discouraged on all grounds. Paint should never be allowed to dry and accumulate on the palette, but it should be scrupulously cleaned away after each using. When there are appreciably large blobs of oil paint worth conserving, some artists collect them with the palette knife, place them on a small sheet of glass or on a saucer and submerge it in a pan of water. The water excludes the action of air and keeps the paint in usable condition. Any drops of water should be allowed to evaporate before replacing these paints on the palette. There is some reasonable doubt as to the advisibility of this ancient and widely used practice because of possible bad effect on the paint.

A great variety of useful water-color palettes, plates and dishes is available in the shops, and here, too, the user must select the kind best suited to his needs. The ancient painters, who made greater use of more fluid paints and lesser use of the pastier ones, used clam shells, small pots and jars to a greater extent than the present painter who usually prefers to spread his paints on the surface where he mixes them. White plastic dinner or soup plates make lightweight and satisfactory fresco palettes.

Mahlstick. The mahlstick is a slender, lightweight inflexible wooden rod about a yard long and generally topped with a small ball which is intended to be padded by tying cloth or chamois around it. The modern ones are usually jointed like a fishing rod and the better ones will have smooth, tight-fitting joints.

The mahlstick is not so universally employed as it was in former times, but it is a most useful implement, especially for those who work in detail or in small forms. Held with the left hand, its end resting on the edge of the painting or against the easel, it makes an effective hand rest so that details, thin lines and carefully placed strokes can be done with greater precision.

GRADES OF ARTISTS' PAINTS

In the artists' supply shops one is usually confronted by a vast array of oil colors, water colors, brushes and other articles, which are confusing not only to the inexperienced but also to some mature painters who have become accustomed to specific brands of goods and are sometimes at a loss to decide, when called upon, to distinguish between unfamiliar makes and varieties.

The advice of all competent authorities and most experienced teachers is that, unless severe financial limitations exist as to make their purchase impossible, none but the very highest grades of colors, brushes, paper, canvas, etc., should ever be chosen either by students or serious painters. The difference between their working or manipulative qualities and those of the inferior grades is so great as to produce entirely different results; it has been noted, for example, in classes where groups of students attempt to work on new techniques, the ones who have brushes of the proper quality usually turn out the best results as far as technical success and paint quality is concerned. The same is true of all other supplies and materials.

Three broad classes of paints are sold by the various artists' material manufacturers. The first- or top-quality professional grade, sold at the highest prices, is supposed to be the finest material the manufacturer can put out—pigments carefully selected from what he honestly believes to be the finest available from world-wide sources; the oils, water-color vehicles or other liquids expertly chosen and compounded according to the most approved procedures. The grinding or other manufacturing operations for a first-rate paint are carried out with conscientious attention to secure the best results, and the entire production is kept under a rigid system of checks and controls.

Preferred brands of paint. For the most part, with hardly any exceptions, the *first-grade* lines of the well-known, widely-distributed American manufacturers comply with these considerations, and the differences between them are more likely to be those of personal judgment than of value since, naturally, there are as many opinions among the paint technicians as to what constitutes a perfect color as there are among artists. When it comes to the finer points, one will find quite a variation; one firm will believe that Indian red should be made of the bluest shade available, another will select an average medium bluish shade. One firm's medium cadmium yellow will be the equivalent of another's deep cadmium yellow and so on. Some painters develop preferences for specific colors and buy one brand of burnt sienna, another make of flake white, etc., whereas others adhere to one entire make.

Furthermore, the top-grade oil colors are now more or less standardized as regard basic, minimum quality. The National

Bureau of Standards has established a set of specifications * to which oil colors should conform, and any tubes of oil paint offered for sale as complying with these specifications, may be relied upon to be of acceptable quality. Paints that exceed these specifications would indeed be superlative in quality. It is hoped that other materials used in serious creative painting will also be regulated by standards established in the same way, through voluntary co-operation between the manufacturers, artists' groups and the government.

In evaluating the products of small, local or new concerns, one must not be too prompt to condemn them, as it is entirely possible to make fine materials commercially on a small scale, and among such we find many entirely satisfactory products. However, it is well to remember that good intentions alone do not make good paints; experience over a long period of years in actual production is requisite, and the lack of sufficient resources to maintain uniformity of materials, experienced personnel, top manufacturing facilities and rigid controls can be a great handicap to efficiency.

Second-grade colors. In addition to the top-grade lines of oil colors and water colors, most of the larger manufacturers also put out a second-grade line under a distinctive trade name. Because there is a large class of users who have small concern with permanence and superior control, these products are an important item in the artists' material trade, probably outselling the finer materials. The better ones among these second-rate products generally brush out well and have fair brilliance and strength, but they are inferior to the top grades. No restrictions or standards exist by which their quality can be controlled. If the manufacturer wants to cheapen a line of colors by using various extenders, or by using lower grade pigments and oils or less expensive grinding methods, it matters little which course he takes; these paints are not made for the utmost in permanence and performance which is expected of materials

---

* Artists' Oil Paints, commercial standard CS98-42. For sale by the Superintendent of Documents, Washington, D. C., price 5¢.

designed for serious creative work and their habitual use is not recommended. For student's exercises, for paintings of a temporary nature or for work intended solely for reproduction their use is justified on the basis of economy.

Student's grade paints. A still lower grade of paints, sold at the lowest prices, is also to be found on the market. These are generally made as cheaply as possible with cost the prime consideration, and consequently they are of inferior quality. The "students' quality" lines often contain imitation colors, impermanent pigments and vehicles, and they are very weak in tinting power. It is doubtful whether their habitual use is justified by serious students, on the theory that training in painting should be carried on with the same or nearly the same professional materials and implements as will be employed in more advanced work.

Modern attitudes on quality. Obviously, fine materials will not make a poor painter great; also no amount of care and success in technical details will make up for the lack of taste or other aesthetic virtues in art. These facts have led to a question in the minds of some painters as to whether the great emphasis placed on extreme qualities of materials and craftsmanship are not overdone; whether the statements of specialists are not a survival of a sort of unnecessary precaution, overrefinement or preciousness. This reasoning is the sort of thing that led to the failures and the low level of technical accomplishment of the recent past. Our current standards are, as a matter of fact, based on a very practical basis. If one compares our present materials with those of former generations of painters, it will be seen that the element of preciousness has been entirely removed; even our most skillfully hand-made products and our superlative grades are turned out in mass-production as compared with the older procedures.

The regular high-grade industrial paints which are produced in bulk are no less carefully manufactured than the finest artists' colors, and although they are formulated to meet different specifications, the procedures for maintenance of quality and uniformity and the methods of control and testing are no different.

The artist of the past always realized that his brushes, colors and canvases were, or should be superlative in quality, and he accepted their greater cost as the necessary price one pays for materials that are beyond the run of the common merchandise of everyday use. The deliberate, habitual use of inferior materials by mature, professional painters is a new trend that has little precedence.

Painting materials in the earliest recorded days were indeed precious things; most of the raw materials were rare, they were obtained at the expense of much labor and they were very costly. In the times of Giotto the colors were treated like jewels and placed upon the paintings with great care. Nowadays we can discard a left-over blob of hardened paint without a qualm, simply because it would be foolish to spend a day's labor to wash out the pigment, purify and regrind it when it can be replaced by clean, fresh material for a few cents. Our best materials are superior to the old grades in every way; they should be handled with the proper respect for their qualities. The use of cheap and inferior grades should be confined to purposes for which they are best suited. As previously indicated, all sorts of inferior materials have been common to all ages and places, and the careful painters of the past have always had to learn how to cope with such conditions.

Books for Additional Reading

The following books may be consulted for more detailed information on the subjects introduced in this book. The first-mentioned title contains a complete, annotated bibliography which should be used by those interested in making a thorough study of any of the topics.

MAYER, RALPH. *The Artists' Handbook of Materials and Techniques,* Viking Press, New York, 1940.

DOERMER, MAX. *The Materials of the Artist and Their Use in Painting,* Harcourt, Brace, New York, 1934.

LAURIE, A. P. *The Painter's Materials and Methods,* Lippincott, Philadelphia, 1926.

INDEX